A Guide to
Getting Work

A Dancer's Guide to Getting Work

Jenny Belingy & John Byrne

A & C Black • London

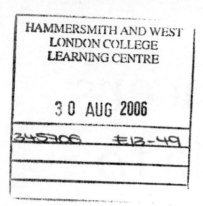
First published 2005
A & C Black Publishers Limited
37 Soho Square, London W1D 3QZ
www.acblack.com

ISBN 0-7136-6946-2

A & C Black uses paper produced with elemental chlorine-free
pulp, harvested from managed sustainable forests.

Typeset in 10 on 12.5pt Sabon
Printed and bound in Great Britain by
Creative Print and Design (Wales), Ebbw Vale

Contents

Foreword

So you want to be a dancer! In that case be prepared for hard work, disappointments, put-downs, aching bones, injuries, physiotherapy bills, pay-cheques that take ages to come in, long hours, backstabbing, cattle-market auditions, endless rehearsals ... well, no-one said it would be easy!

But a truly worthwhile career can be achieved in the world of dance, if you have the strength and determination – both more important, even, than physical aptitude and technique.

When I began dancing at the age of 17 – far too late, I was told, because I had no turn-out – I did not expect to be still dancing now, or to be working as one of the top choreographers in London, let alone in the country. Coming from a working-class family who did not fulfil any of their dreams, and growing up listening to my parents telling me what they 'coulda, shoulda, woulda', I started out on a journey which changed the rest of my life. Moving to London with only £50 in my pocket, I began to scout around for agents, classes – anything that would get my foot in the door ... a door which was slammed in my face many times, for one reason or another.

I was on the point of giving up, believing that I was just one little fish in a big pond, when confidence, belief, and a sense of individuality all kicked in – and I was a new person. All doubts were thrown aside and I started to believe that dancing was the only thing I wanted to do for the rest of my life. Just as a cat stretches first thing in the morning, it became my daily routine, whether I was sick, tired or injured. Of course, I discovered that just as important as having talent was the ability to be in the right place at the right time.

For me, dancing is personal; a way of expressing my true self. I get a kick out of it when I'm down; it makes me feel good, keeps me fit, and it's something that no-one can take away. Also, I'm doing something different – something not many people in London do, and something I really enjoy while getting paid for it too. I get to travel and see the world. I'm my own boss, work my own hours, and meet some really nice people (as well as some not so nice!). It's never dull.

So what are you waiting for?

Be strong, be honest with yourself, keep an open mind, take in as many styles and opportunities as you can, and never stop learning. By following the expert guidance given by the authors of, and contributors to, this book, and by dancing from the heart, you will have the best possible chance of enjoying a rewarding and fulfilling career in this exciting creative field. Most of all, be yourself – and enjoy.

Dennis Wonder
December 2004

Dedication & Acknowledgements

Jenny: I dedicate this book to my nephew Kyle and niece Jasmine (aka Petunia) and all of my god children. You are the future and this book illustrates that no matter who you are or what age, always go with your heart's desire and follow your DESTINY. My thanks go out to God first and foremost – if I didn't rely on his strength this could not have happened. Family? You have been there for me during the rough and the smooth. Denize thanks for the ear and use of your laptop. Mum thank you for sending me to ballet!!! I'd also like to thank Uncle Pert, Tony and Aunt Joyce not forgetting AJ, my Godmother Auntie Joan, Sahra, Wendy A, Andrew, Karen, Sharon A, Diane, Aneta, Geo, Janet Bailey, Duncan and Carl Williams, John and all who attended London's Victory. Never be afraid to step into your calling, be happy in the career you choose.

John: My dedication is to my parents Charles and Eileen Byrne, the most famous dancers in Ireland (well, to us anyhow!) and my thanks go to Jenny for (as usual) reminding me of all the people who needed thanking!

Introduction

Any book which claimed to be the definitive guide to its particular subject would be dancing on dangerous ground – so that's a claim we want to distance ourselves from right from the start.

There are many, many books available on the history, theory, practice and appreciation of dance. This book was written simply because, while Jenny built her dance career and John developed his practice as career adviser and 'agony uncle' for *The Stage* newspaper, one of the things that seemed to inflict the most agony on beginners was the lack of information on how to build a dance career. Aware that the best way to put all their 'book learning' into practice would be to apply it in a work environment, they were finding advice on how to take those vital first steps into the dance world hard to come by. Attempting to address this need, we have written this book to help the beginner who is hoping to break into the dance world, and may not as yet have many contacts in that environment. However, it should also be of use to more experienced performers and to dancers who work in pairs (ballroom or salsa dancers, for instance).

Many of the principles and attitudes we describe are the same ones that most seasoned professional dancers use to build their careers over decades. Or to put it another way, when something goes *wrong* in a top dancer's career, it is not usually because the dancer has invented some highly original error that is only possible with years of experience – it is more likely that the star has neglected something very basic.

Equally, the strength of a dance team is based on the strength of the individual members. In some chapters, such as those dealing with auditions or performing, the same attitudes and encouragement we have recommended for the individual dancer will work for the dancer in a team or in a partnership, too. The information in other chapters, for example on marketing and business practice, can very easily be adapted to work for marketing and running a dance team as well.

With so many different styles of dance and types of dance

professional, from the classical ballet star to the streetdance diva, we have tried to focus on the general principles of career success rather than to dwell in too much detail on any one style. At the same time we have drawn on a wide range of examples to illustrate our points.

Our aim is to provide the reader with a basic approach to career-building which will get them moving up the ladder fast, systematically and with the confidence that whatever knowledge and experience they need to make it to the very top is already within their grasp.

In effect, our goal is to duplicate the same teaching techniques that Jenny uses in her classes and John applies in his coaching: the 'secret' of success is actually no big secret at all. Rather, it is for each individual dancer to become aware of his or her unique talents and abilities and to build on the strengths they already possess.

Building on that success can be done in two ways. The first is through practice, perseverance and hard work – and no book can do that for you. But while there's no way round the 'sweating and stretching' aspect of becoming a top dancer, there are certainly ways to speed up the process and get maximum value from the work you put in.

Which leads us to success method number two: while each dancer has their own unique and individual style, many thousands of dancers before you have worked their way up the same career ladder. And the ones who have been most successful have tended to employ the same principles and techniques. In putting this book together we have been able to tap into the knowledge and experience of some very successful names in the business, alongside our own track record in supporting many different performers to reach their goals. Of course, the one thing we don't know at this point is what *your* particular goals are for your dance career. Do you know them yourself?

If not, before you start working through the book we'd like to encourage you to start thinking about where you aim to end up. Have you always dreamed of being a dancer but never been quite sure what kind of training you need? Or maybe you know exactly what you need to learn but just haven't quite plucked up the courage to put your plans into action. Maybe you started out on your dance career a few years ago and got sidetracked or disappointed when things didn't quite go your way ... or perhaps you are looking at the end of your dancing days and would like one shot at creating and promoting the kind of dance show that truly expresses who you are, before you hang up your shoes.

Alternatively, you may never have thought about where your career might take you, beyond the general desire to make a living from doing the thing you love. Take some time now to explore in your imagination how it would feel to be at the peak of your dancing career. What would that look like for you? Would you be performing to sell-out audiences? Would you be watching yourself take centre stage in the hottest dance videos by the world's biggest music stars? Maybe your dream is to take your place as a member of an internationally renowned dance company, or perhaps dance is just one of your talents and you intend to use it to kick-start a multi-faceted showbusiness career.

The more you can focus on your career vision, the more you can work out what steps you need to take right now to start making it a reality. Chances are you'll find that the most immediate steps are already within your grasp. You'll certainly find all the information in this book to help you take those steps – or at the very least, links to some great resources to help you discover that information.

Whatever your dancing dreams, we hope you find something in here to inspire, educate and encourage you. And we hope you'll keep us informed of the progress of your dance career – if something works for you, we'd be delighted to hear about it so that we can recommend it to more people. And if something doesn't work, we'll still be pleased to hear that you gave it a try. The courage to 'have a go' is one of the big factors in making the most of your dance abilities. Finally, when you end up as a top working dancer, don't forget to let us know the discoveries you made on the way there – so that we can include them in a future edition of this book.

Every dancer's journey is different, but every journey starts out with a love of dance and a dream to step into. We're really looking forward to taking these next steps on your journey right alongside you!

Jenny Belingy
John Byrne

Chapter One

Taking the First Step

Dance lessons for beginners ... and for
professionals too

The importance of dance training

What skills really make a successful dancer? Perseverance must
be pretty near the top of the list: forging a successful career in
any area of showbusiness takes time. Lots of energy? That goes
without saying – and you can throw in the ability to focus that
energy, too. Sometimes you'll need to focus it in several
directions at the same time, especially at the beginning of your
career when you may need to organise your dancing around
your 'day job'. But what about your actual dancing ability?

John has worked with a lot of singers, at every level of career
success – and as well as her dance talents, Jenny has had some
outings as a singer, too. While we would never suggest that
building a singing career is any easier than building a dance
career, one thing we have both observed is that it isn't always
the singers with the most technically perfect voices who have
had the most success. Helped by a striking image, a good choice
of songs, perhaps the ability to 'talk' the lyrics in a style that
sounds like singing, and ever-increasing leaps in recording and
backing-track technology, many 'singers' with fairly average
voices – and even some who don't have very good voices at all
– can still make it in the music industry.

With dancing, though, what you see is pretty much what you
get. While *Matrix*-style slow-motion and exciting camera angles
can certainly spice up a routine in a music video, the dancer
needs to be able to perform the basic moves to make it all work.
In fact, for many 'special effects' type camera set-ups, a dancer
often has to exercise extreme precision and movement control
or the expensive technology will be useless.

It's also true that even if you spend every weekend dancing at the hottest clubs in town, social or recreational dancing won't prepare you for the rigours of a professional dance career, any more than a Sunday kick-around would prepare a football player for the Premier League. Training is one of the major ongoing factors in any dance career, especially since most of that career may well be spent 'training' for one thing or another. For one job you might find yourself busting a move in the latest 'street dance' style; for the next, you may spend eight months rediscovering the Charleston or the Black Bottom for a period show like *Thoroughly Modern Millie*.

And these days, of course, even 'period' shows often incorporate more contemporary styles into their choreography. As for styles like disco or salsa which 'everybody can do', the audience are paying you and the director to come up with variations that they *haven't* seen before – so the more styles you brush up on in your own time, the more you'll be able to offer the choreographer at audition time. We'll be talking in detail about your health and welfare later in the book, but it is worth mentioning here that not only does training help to get your skills up to a level where you can earn a living from them, it is also an important factor in getting your body to the level of fitness you'll need to be a working dancer.

If, however, you are reading this and haven't had any dance training to date, don't despair. Contrary to popular belief, you don't necessarily have to have signed on with a Ballet Academy from the time you were three to have any hope of making it as a dancer. The more dance training you have done in the past, the less basic training you will need now – but, as with any other kind of training, the success of your own programme chiefly depends on how much time you are prepared to put into it now, rather than how much experience you have had in the past.

And how much time you are prepared to put into it now very much depends on how serious you are about pursuing your dancing career. In this, as in most other branches of showbusiness, the 'I'll wait until I'm successful and then really work hard' attitude doesn't hold much water. If you have the opposite attitude – a love of dance and a desire to be the best dancer *you* can be (as opposed to comparing yourself to others) – it's never too late to start. You may not pull it off ... but even that feels a lot better than spending your life wondering what would have happened if you'd tried. One of our aims in this book is to remove some of the mystery from that 'if'. But while we can give you the information you need, we can't come round to your house and force you to put that information into practice. Even if we could, we would probably have to go round to every single reader's house, because each dancer has different strengths and weaknesses, styles and personalities.

For all these reasons, there is no substitute for proper dance training with a good teacher to give you the foundation for building a successful career. Just as there are self-taught actors and musicians, so there are self-taught dancers – and it's true that some of them do make it in the dance world. In general, though, relying totally on yourself will tend to limit the opportunities available to you, both in terms of finding work and in terms of stretching your abilities and becoming the best dancer you can be. Even the most die-hard self-taught performers usually realise this eventually and, when they have a little more finance available, start to train in ways that will expand what they already know. Not only does the new training not 'cramp their style' (the big fear of every self-taught artist!), it often allows them to fulfil even more of their vision than they had previously thought possible.

Fortunately you don't have to wait until you become a megastar to get quality dance training. In fact, there are usually lots of opportunities to acquire that training, no matter what stage of your career you are at or where you live. From morning classes at the local community centre to fully fledged dance studios, from part-time courses to full-time colleges, you may be surprised by the variety of teaching available once you start to look. There are some very good teachers out there, too. Many talented professional dancers turn to teaching when they scale down their own performing careers, while many working dancers also teach to supplement their income. In both cases, you – the student – get the chance to draw not just on their knowledge of the basics of dance training, but also on their invaluable experience of working as a dancer in the real world. Of course, as in any other profession, the best practitioners don't necessarily make the best teachers, and time and budget will also be factors in the kind of dance training that will work best for you at this stage in your career. What *will* be the deciding factor is not so much the quality of the class or teacher, but the level of your own commitment to get the most out of your training so that it really sets you up for your future career.

The 'commitment factor' is sufficiently important for us to spend a little more time clarifying what it actually means. We have already used the analogy of a football career to talk about the difference between recreational/social dancing and dancing which is targeted at finding work. It is very important to be clear, at the outset of your dance training, that what you are aiming for is *a career*. While there is nothing more enjoyable than doing something you love and getting paid for it, if dancing is just an interest or a hobby for you, you are probably better keeping it as just that. You can then do as many or as few fun classes as you enjoy or can afford. If you are really committed to forging a career, you will still enjoy training, but only if you appreciate that the amount and intensity of work involved will be way beyond what a mere hobby or interest would require.

The kind of training you choose will depend on your own ambitions, the options available to you locally, and the size of your budget. And we hope that fun and enjoyment, friendships and fulfilment will also be part of your training experience. However, it's only fair to point out that if you don't feel like you are working hard – and even *too* hard, on occasion – you are probably not putting in the kind of effort necessary to properly compete for dance jobs. Many teachers would recommend that you don't even consider applying for dance work until you have at least one year of consistent training under your belt. There are a couple of reasons why that advice makes sense: for one thing, if the audition goes badly it can affect your confidence (and the competition for dance jobs these days is so intense that there will almost certainly be many highly trained dancers going for the same position). But even if the 'Hollywood' scenario comes to pass and you end up 'blagging' your way into a job, it's unlikely that you would do well. To use the football analogy again, a Sunday team might last one match in the Premier League, and perhaps even do well, if the wind was with them; but sustaining a whole season of matches at that level wouldn't just show up their lack of experience – it would quite possibly kill them! Dance training is very much a two-way process. From your teacher and school you are looking for the techniques and moves that will help you express yourself in the way you want to, and in a way that audiences will want to pay to watch. But the stamina and fitness needed to put those moves and techniques into practice are qualities you have to look for within yourself, and can only be built up through discipline and time.

Two types of dancer

In this chapter we are going to assume that there are two basic kinds of dancer. The first kind has probably already been studying dance for some time, perhaps since childhood. If this is you, you're unlikely to need much convincing of the benefits of dance training – and you may well already be aware of the kind of further dance training that is available. Good children's teachers and courses are always happy to recommend further education to build on the sound foundations that have already been laid.

If you are now embarking on a serious career plan, you certainly won't have to put in as much basic groundwork as someone who is starting later, and you will have the luxury of being able to choose and focus on the ideal top-up and complementary skills to increase your marketability as a dancer. The guidelines listed in the following pages will help you choose the best-quality courses and get the most for your money, but the most valuable thing that you can do to move forwards will be to really work on that career vision we talked about in the introduction to this book. When you know where you ultimately want to end up in your career, you can make better decisions about which courses you should be doing now to help you get there.

The second kind of dancer who may be leafing through these pages is likely to be someone who has always loved dance and enjoyed dancing; perhaps somebody whose dancing has often been commented on by other people. Although they may have some degree of dance learning – perhaps they have done a night class or are members of a club – it has so far been sporadic and enjoyed principally as a hobby. They may have undertaken some formal dance training at an earlier age, but for whatever reason this wasn't sustained. Nevertheless the desire to get more serious about a dance career is burning strongly and it's time to get serious about this business.

As we have already said, it is never too late to fulfil your passion. So let's look at a dance training plan that starts from scratch and, depending on which of the two reader types you most resemble, you can identify your own most likely starting point.

Researching your training

Before you decide on the course you want to pursue, your first step should be to research what training is available. You should take some time in doing this – after all, you are aiming to make a long-term commitment to dancing, so you want to choose from as wide a range of options as possible. In our resource section (see pp. 127–34) you'll find several websites, publications and organisations that can help you discover what's available in your local area (and perhaps what might be available further afield, but might excite you enough to travel for).

Your local library or adult education centre is always a good option, especially if your research has to be done on a limited budget. Of course, there's no substitute for actual experience – so if you happen to know anyone in the dance business, either working as a dancer or studying to be one, it's certainly worth sounding them out to see what suggestions they may have. At some time in their own careers they'll have been where you are now, and the majority of professional dancers will be only too happy to share their experiences with you if you demonstrate that you are serious.

If there are famous or successful dancers who have inspired you, there can be no harm in dropping them a note – care of their agent, if you can find out who that is – or through their website if they have one. Again, a few simple, practical questions rather than a long, gushy fan letter are likely to yield the best and most useful results. One of the most useful questions to ask is where and how they did their own training, and what they would do differently if they were starting out again. You will find that the majority of dancers have had formal college training in dance, and we will talk about this in more detail shortly. But let's say that perhaps because of finances, or time or some other constraint, a full-time course isn't possible for you at the moment. It may also be that you would prefer a taste of dance tuition before you really commit to moving forwards in your career. You will then be looking at whatever part-time courses are open to you.

Part-time training

In some cases, the dance colleges which run full-time courses also run part-time courses with qualifications. For many people – particularly mature students with family or other commitments – this can be a very useful option ... although it follows, of course, that the necessary levels of fitness/stamina will take longer to achieve on a part-time course than on a full-time one.

If you are considering part-time dance training, the key factor to bear in mind is whether the course you are signing up for is mainly recreational, or one which offers a proper grounding in professional dance techniques. A class or course with more general appeal may be less expensive, but it should be obvious that it won't come close to being a foundation on which you can build a career. (In fairness to many perfectly competent social dance or aerobics teachers, they may never have claimed to be providing anything other than a fun class; such teachers should not have to face the wrath of dissatisfied 'serious' dancers halfway through the course simply because those dancers failed to read the course description properly.) Check the course information thoroughly to make sure you don't get your hopes up, only to end up disappointed and out of pocket.

On the other hand, if it really has been some time since you wore your dancing shoes, it is a good idea to start off slowly to ensure that the class you join is at the right level for your ability. Throwing yourself into an advanced class for the first time may not be advisable; it will take time to get into the rhythm of things, and you don't want to knock your confidence before you even get going.

As well as adult education centres and community-orientated courses, you may want to find out if there is a professional dance studio near you. Unlike a school hall, a professional studio will be fully kitted-out with the full-length mirrors and special flooring required for practising dance at the highest level. It will tend to host courses and classes for professional dancers and to hire out spaces for professional shows and auditions. Don't automatically assume, because it is a studio for dance professionals, that it won't hold beginners' classes (or that the classes will be radically more expensive than other courses) – but equally, be aware that participants on the majority of courses are likely to be trained dancers. As a beginner you may find it difficult to keep up, and the tutors may not have the time to give repeat instructions for fear of holding up other people in the class. On the other hand, if you would like a challenge and are prepared to work hard, knowing that you can hold your own in a class full of professional dancers will certainly increase your confidence in your own career potential. And being in the company of professionals is bound to give you the chance to pick up lots of tips and information of the sort which can only be learned from experience. A further advantage is that studio dance classes are often scheduled so that you can go from one to another, polishing up several aspects of your dancing at the same time.

Whichever venue you choose for your training, the best way to be sure that a class 'fits' is to see if you can negotiate a free or reduced-rate taster session before you commit to signing up. Many teachers and classes offer such sessions as a matter of course, especially in September and January (traditionally the beginning of 'night class' season). If such an offer isn't forth-coming, there's no reason why you shouldn't suggest it – after all, if you don't ask, you don't get. Even if you don't get to take part in a class, you may be allowed to sit in as an observer – and if you're itching to be involved by the end of the class, that's a very good sign.

Another way to see if a dance class lives up to its publicity is to keep an eye out for 'showcase' performances. Sometimes these are geared towards bringing the school to the attention of potential new clients; other shows are aimed more at giving existing students the chance to show what they have learned to family and friends. On formal courses, the showcases also create an opportunity for graduates to display their wares to agents and others who might be able to bring them work. If you can get to one of these performances, it will give you a chance to see what kind of standard you could hope to achieve with the school's help (although obviously, the quality of work will be down to the talent of individual students too). It will certainly give you the opportunity to chat to some of the existing students and see what their advice is.

Learning the basics of dance is one thing, but you will also be looking to pull all your knowledge and skill together with panache and flair. A dance teacher or studio which brings this quality to its end-of-year showcase is certainly one worth considering. Be sure to check out the teacher's own qualifications, dance background and previous teaching experience. Feel free to ask questions: a good teacher will have no objection to answering them. For instance, you might enquire what age of student and styles of dance they specialise in teaching, and how long they have been teaching for. Just as you enjoy dancing, teachers are usually involved in it because they love it too – so it is also in their interest to have students in their classes who will actually enjoy being there.

Get an idea of how much progress the tutor feels you can make – and in how many classes. We know that this depends to some extent on the individual student, but even if you can get the teacher to give you a rough idea of what is possible, it will give you a guideline as to whether this is the right school or course for you. In other words, it will prevent either you or your teacher from having unrealistic expectations of what you can achieve with the time and resources you have available. We have already cautioned against jumping into a class that is too far above your level to begin with; but besides ability, you also need to think about the time you have available for training, and other such factors. If you are serious about working as a dancer, you will want to work with a teacher who stretches you a little. Signing up for a course that requires work over several nights a week when you can only manage one may demoralise more than it helps you, especially if you find yourself falling behind the more regular students. One way to keep a check on your progress is self-assessment: a good tutor will encourage this, and you might even consider getting someone to video you from time to time. As you watch the tapes you should notice continuous improvement month-on-month. If you don't, and assuming you are keeping your practice up, it may be time to find a new approach or perhaps a new teacher.

As with any other service, you are entitled to expect good professional conduct from your dance teacher – whether they operate out of the local community centre, in a college or in their own personal studio. There should be a sense of progression in the lessons, and even if there are one or two 'stars' in the class, every student should feel that they are getting their fair share of attention. Checking on your dance teacher's qualifications and membership of professional bodies is one way to try and ensure that you've chosen the right person, but it is also true that even if the teacher is a good one, there are occasions on which a pupil and teacher just don't 'gel'.

As we have already noted, most dance teachers are very serious about what they do and committed to supporting their students. So if you feel you are struggling in class, do be brave enough to raise it; if the problem can't be solved, your teacher may be able to recommend another class – and if it's in the same centre, your fees might be transferable.

On the rarer occasions when the teacher is not running things to professional standards, don't be shy about insisting on getting what you are paying for. Again, it is fair to take up any problems with the teacher first, but if you get no satisfaction you may need to go to the course director. If the training establishment is a reputable one, they should be sufficiently concerned to get the problem sorted out amicably – preferably without disrupting your dance studies, but at the very least by giving you a refund. As a beginner in showbusiness, you might be shy of sticking up for yourself in case you ruin your reputation. But, while nobody likes someone who is difficult for no reason, the nature of being a dancer is that you will need to develop a reasonably thick skin. In any case, nobody is going to blame you for standing up for your rights if you have a good reason.

Speaking of value for money, think hard about the cost of the course you are doing versus the amount of teaching time you are getting. Some tutors and classes offer a 'pay as you go' option, but if you are a member of a studio or a gym then there may well be discount options if you book a set number of classes in advance. It's certainly true that paying out in advance is a great motivation to keep up the classes, when muscles you haven't used in some time begin to ache! Although a school that is close to you may make for cheaper transport costs, it is better to base your decision on the quality of the tuition, so that you get value for your money in the long run. Other factors, such as the cleanliness of the facilities and the state of the changing rooms, may well affect your decision – after all, you will learn better in a place where you are comfortable. On the other hand, we can tell you from personal experience that as a professional performer, not all the venues you will experience will conform to the same high standards!

So far we have worked on the assumption that you are looking to join a class of some sort. However, we sometimes get asked if one-to-one dance tuition would be a better option. It is certainly true that as dancers begin to build their professional reputation, they may invest in one-to-one classes with a specialist trainer in order to develop a particular style of dance – and especially styles which involve working as a couple, like salsa or ballroom, where bringing in an objective eye can certainly help to polish that 'killer routine'. At the beginning of a dance career, though, we feel that taking part in a class situation has more benefits. For one thing, the majority of your career is going to involve working with other performers, be it as part of a dance troupe or as part of a show. Since people in general, and performers in particular, are such a varied and volatile bunch, it makes great sense to get used to working with them in all their vast variety as early as possible.

Most people who have been through a creative education of any sort would agree that, while there is a lot we can learn from a great tutor, we can also learn a great deal from the different styles and approaches of other people we study with. Watching what they do well, and watching what they do wrong, can both be a great help in developing our own learning and dancing style. Moreover, one-to-one tuition by its very nature will make a much larger dent in your pocket than learning in a class. Quite often you will have to pay not just for the teacher's time, but also for the use of the studio space. By the time you *do* want individual attention, it is better to have a lot of class hours under your belt so that you know exactly what you want to achieve and can get maximum value from your investment.

Where extra training may come in handy – in conjunction with your regular dance work – is in the area of special skills. As choreographers work ceaselessly to make their routines exciting and contemporary, they are increasingly fond of throwing other moves into the mix. From martial arts to circus skills, from juggling to skateboarding, any 'secret weapons' you can hone during your training time may well give you the extra edge in some future audition. Don't neglect any language skills you may have picked up at school – even if you never saw any use for them up until now. You don't necessarily have to speak other languages to travel as a dancer: performance is, after all, a universal language. But cultural capitals like Paris and Barcelona, and the many French- and Spanish-speaking countries around the world, can also be hotbeds of performance work. A working knowledge of another language will certainly increase your chances of employment, if only in being able to read the job ads!

Full-time training

While it is perfectly possible to learn enough from part-time classes to build your career, few dancers would argue that the best start is to study dance or performing arts full-time – either straight after school, or as a mature student. There are numerous courses and colleges to choose from (see the resource section at the back of this book for details), and what could be better than spending all day studying a subject that you love? And you had *better* love dancing, because whatever full-time course you choose, you will be in for a lot of hard work! The first year of any performance course is usually the time when people discover whether what they thought was a lifelong dream was actually just a fantasy.

While part-time dance training allows you to sample the various dance styles and build up your versatility, full-time training is more likely to mean that you specialise in one partic-ular area as you complete your course. It makes sense that if you are putting time, expense and energy into studying dance full-time, you will want to get the maximum return on your invest-ment and become as good as you possibly can. For this reason you will need a clear vision of your future direction so you can select the appropriate course of study (see Chapter Two for a good range of options to consider, if you haven't made that choice already). A three-year course in ballet won't be the best option if what you actually love is musical theatre, any more than your tap-dancing skills will make you welcome in a production of *Swan Lake*. In general, most dance courses focus on ballet, contemporary dance or musical theatre, although ethnic dance-forms from Flamenco to South Asian dance are increasingly turning up on college schedules. And although you will be aiming to excel in your chosen field of study, it is becoming more common for the career-minded dancer to study an additional major dance style to a professional level of proficiency – so now you see why full-time dance courses are hard work!

No matter how much your heart is set on going to a particular school – perhaps one you have seen on TV or one that a dancer you admire has attended – it makes sense to study more than one prospectus closely. At your admissions interview you may well find yourself fielding questions about why you have chosen to apply to that particular college, or to study that particular style; good dance tutors will be just as anxious as you that you should end up on the right course. If you don't get into the college you were hoping for, it may not necessarily be because you weren't talented enough. It may just be that the admissions team have decided that your talents would best blossom elsewhere.

The most common types of full-time dance training are three-year diploma courses and four-year degree courses. Each course is different, but normally the diploma courses place the emphasis on the physical side of dancing. While you get just as much physical activity in a degree course, you will also put in extra study on the academic side of the business, with dance theory, history and hopefully some career training on the menu. Your desire at the beginning may be to dance, dance, dance – but be aware that academic qualifications can make it possible for you to get a much wider range of jobs both inside and outside the dance world. Your academic work can also be a big help when you finally give up dancing, whether that happens voluntarily or through other circumstances such as an accident. Sadly, the best training in the world can't completely immunise you against such a possibility – but a good dance course will certainly aim to give you coping skills if something unfortunate were to occur.

One of the first things you will learn on your dance course is stamina. Classes will start early in the morning and go on till late in the evening. You will normally start off with ballet work (even if you are aiming for a career in contemporary dance or musical theatre), so that the stretching and posture exercises set you up for the day. The rest of the day will see you moving from class to class and teacher to teacher for a varied timetable of lessons and workouts.

No matter how qualified a teacher or reputable a college you pick, the main factor in the success of your training is, of course, *you*. Turning up on time for classes, doing the prescribed home-work, making an effort to give your best to all of the instruction – even the parts that don't excite or interest you all that much ... the habits you develop during your training will set the pattern for your behaviour throughout your dance career. In some cases they will determine whether you are going to have a career at all.

While you may envy the working dancer who is constantly getting called for new and exciting jobs, remember that in order to keep working, a dancer often has to do what they are told rather than being totally free to experiment and discover their individual gifts for themselves. Your years of training are the time when you really have that freedom, so work hard and make the most of them.

By the time you finish your dance training you will be strong, flexible, fit and ready to make all the sweating and aching you've done along the way pay off. As the famous choreo-grapher Debbie Allen used to say in the *Fame* TV show, 'You want fame? Well, Fame costs!' At the beginning of this chapter we recommended that you get some training done before you start seriously looking for work. You may well now have selected a course of study ... but we hope that you will still continue on to the next chapter. Just as every decision you make in your training should be based on what you ultimately hope to achieve as a dancer, so – to help you see the various roads you may choose to travel on the way to your ultimate destination – we have signposted some career options of the most popular dancers (and also some more unusual ones that you may not have considered). You may well find that having seen where you want to go, the best course to get you there becomes a lot more obvious.

Chapter Two

Life's a Dance

A guide to your career options

As we have already mentioned, most working dancers operate in one or more of three distinct fields: ballet, contemporary dance or musical theatre. Having said that, the norm is to specialise in one field and to have a good working knowledge of the others. Ask any working dancer how they have made a living over the past decade and you may well discover a surprising and fascinating list of jobs – not all of them dance-related. In this chapter we aim to provide an overview of the most common work areas for dancers. We hope that in doing so we can give you a few insights into the skills required for areas you may already be considering, so you can decide if you need to develop those areas of your training and practice. Equally, we have tried to cast our net wide and touch on a few areas you may not have considered before.

As we progress through our chapters on self-marketing and the dance business, we will be reminding you that when it comes to being a working dancer, your brain is just as important an element of your toolbox as your feet. With this in mind, the focus of this chapter will be more on the contemporary dance and musical theatre aspects of dance careers. While classical ballet is certainly a lively and viable career field for the dancer – just as much as it is an art form – this area of dance does have a slightly more formal training and career-advancement structure, which to cover in the detail required would fill a book in itself. In fact, there are several very good books and websites which will provide you with a wealth of information on classical ballet if this is the area you have your heart set on, and we have done our best to list some particularly useful ones in our resource section. Bear in mind that a lot of mythology and stuffiness has grown up around what is or isn't possible in a ballet career; you'll find that like all working performers, serious ballet professionals don't have time to get sidetracked by such myths and rumours, and neither should you. We encourage you to make good use of the information resources provided, and to make sound career decisions based on the facts. And even if ballet is your dream, we would also encourage you to read through the rest of this chapter before you shoot off to the resource section. Like any other dance career, a ballet career takes time and money to build, and many top dancers have supplemented their income by working in more 'commercial' fields from time to time.

Similarly, as audiences become more discerning, and as technology makes cultural events and styles which were once the exclusive province of those 'in the know' available to a global audience, the lines between contemporary dance and musical theatre are becoming less rigid. Both these dance areas cover a wide range of expressions, events and dance styles, from the huge commercial smash-hit to the small, personal show that just about covers its costs.

Perhaps when you are finishing a 40-date, two-continent tour as the featured dancer with the latest hip-hop megastar, your thoughts won't be so much about your next gig as they will about putting your feet up by the pool (or possibly soaking them *in* the pool). However, at the beginning of your dance career you will probably be happy to grab any dance job going – for the experience, as much as for the money. We would certainly encourage you to try a range of different avenues (with one or two exceptions which we'll cover later), and so we have compiled a list of the main dance career options. These are given in no particular order, but are limited to those areas in which people are making money. Even if you do – as we hope – make it to the top of your own chosen dance ladder, you will probably find yourself running through this list of options several times over the next couple of years. As we often say to performers, what you are ultimately aiming for is not just one good gig, or even a whole string of successful gigs. Read on to see where *your* career might take you.

Music videos and live shows

Not so long ago, most performers just embarking on their professional career would list a TV spot as their ultimate goal.

Dancers were no exception: just as appearing on *Top of the Pops* used to be the yardstick by which singers and musicians measured their career success, so groups like Hot Gossip and Pan's People introduced the concept of dancers and dance groups as stars in their own right to audiences of the 1970s and 1980s. In one sense, dance today has become even more integral to the music and TV industries; no new music release seems complete without its quota of gyrating dancers. In another way, though, the many advances in visual technology since the days of terrestrial-only television have made for big changes in the dance market – and in TV career options.

Certainly there are still chances to get on TV, but dance as the central focus of a TV spot is becoming more and more rare (except on some specialist arts channels). Instead, dance has become one of the major visual props of the music industry, and if you do show up on screen it is just as likely to be on video as live in the studio. Moreover, dancers are no longer the only people in the business doing the dancing: these days, many more singers are required to show off their own dance moves for their teeny fans. The carefully choreographed 'amateur' steps of the latest pop idol need to be supported by seriously good dancing from their posse, and it is still possible for a dancer like Jennifer Lopez to step from the background into the limelight and on to become a diva in her own right.

Of course the nature of video production is such that, as music stars flit back and forth across the globe promoting their latest single before it crashes out of the charts (and at the time of writing this may be less than a fortnight after it is released), it is often impractical for the same team of dancers used in the video to come along for the ride. Therefore, once you break into the music scene, you can find yourself being asked to dance with a wide range of different, often very famous, artists at short notice.

It makes sense, then, that just as a function singer needs to keep up-to-date with all the latest and most popular songs, so you need to make it your business not just to become an expert in the latest sounds, but also in the dance moves that go with them. With manufactured bands being more overtly in the forefront of music, you could even find yourself joining a band – since the increasing importance of visuals means that singing and musical skills are sometimes not the most important element of the product. Good miming skills have landed several dancers their moment of glory in the pop charts!

One way to break into the music business is to hook up with an up-and-coming band at the point where they are working the club circuit to build their reputation (or the secondary school circuit, if they are targeting the youth market). At this stage in their career there may not be a huge amount of money floating around – although you should get paid for your services. However, having dancers on board can give a breaking band a much-needed appearance of glamour and cool when they can't afford a flashy video. It would be nice to say that if the band goes on to have a hit record, they will carry you to fame along with them, but sadly the music industry isn't famous for its loyalty. Your best bet for staying on board is to be so good at what you do, and so in tune with what the bands you back are trying to achieve, that they would be out of their minds to pick anyone else. Dance like you are playing the BRIT Awards when you are still on the club-and-pub circuit, and you might just end up dancing there for real.

If the band you are working with has any record-industry backing at all, you will almost certainly find yourself dancing on TV – although it is likely to be a local cable station or a Saturday morning kids' show. The first thing you will learn is that TV studios are a lot more cramped inside then they look on screen. A good pointer to remember is that TV and live dancing are almost the exact opposite of each other in terms of the movements you need to make. By its very nature, television work is quite 'close up', especially in the kind of small basement studios that many music and children's shows are shot in. Therefore you need to reign in your movements accordingly while still holding on to the energy and general look of the song's video, if there is one. Big 'live stage' moves look too exaggerated on camera, and if you're not careful you might knock over some equipment, which certainly won't increase your chances of being asked back.

In general, whether you are dancing in a TV studio or on the set of a video, you will be well treated and supplied with food, make-up and cars to pick you up and drop you. And of course you get to meet and dance with the stars up close. While most dancers we know have their favourites, and there are the occasional nightmares, most stars got where they are by hard work and professionalism, and this is what they admire in and expect from other people whom they work with. It is not by any means uncommon to find yourself 'chilling' with a world-famous face between takes, and on world tours it has even happened that romance has blossomed between a star and their dancer!

However, the key word in working in the music business is professionalism. Behind the rock-and-roll image lies an obsession with number-crunching, and such cardinal sins as getting star-struck and over-familiar with a star, or being late or unprepared and holding up a screamingly expensive shoot, are likely to send you back to the pub circuit faster than a teenager forgets last week's chart record. Keep your focus and don't be distracted: many music videos are very intricate operations with long shoots and multiple takes. Not only might you have to perform the same routine over and over again, you might also have to do it in an extremely 'stop/start' fashion, so that a strong sense of focus and stamina is very important for this kind of work.

Due to changing musical trends, music can sometimes become a hit without a band or singer being involved at all. In clubs at home and on the continent, DJ mixes often become the hottest tracks around, and you may find yourself employed to provide the visuals by dancing on the stage while the track is played through the speakers – a task that is sometimes called 'fronting'. (It has been suggested that this might be because performing in venues full of frenzied clubbers requires a lot of 'front', but the reality is that you are an important factor in the track's success and should expect to be well-looked-after by the promotion company.) The very successful pop group Steps supposedly owed its existence to a team of dancers who were put together to front, of all things, a line-dance record.

An important point to keep in mind when working in the music industry is that you are normally there as a support artist. While you should always do your best in every dance job, some-times this is as much about being in control of your talent as letting it loose at full blast. You might be the world's greatest singer, but if you are working as a backing vocalist you won't get any thanks for out-singing the lead singer, no matter how off-key they might be. Equally, as a dancer your job is to do your best while making even the most flatfooted pop star look like they were born to dance. Darlene Love, who *is* known as the world's best backing vocalist, once told John that the secret of her success is that she can sing with anyone and make them sound good. If you can develop a similar attitude to your dancing you may well create a similar niche for yourself in the music world.

Although variety and light-entertainment-style television has yet to make its predicted comeback, there are still occasions on which dancers and dance routines feature in live and pre-recorded TV shows. For instance, big TV 'events' like *Comic Relief* or *Children in Need* often open with production numbers, while shows like *Stars In Their Eyes* use professional dancers to add to the authenticity of imitation superstars. When *Come Dancing* was revived in its celebrity version, real ballroom dancers were partnered with the star contestants to help teach them the steps.

Although a TV show with a studio audience won't have quite as many stops and starts as a video shoot, it can be a little off-putting for the beginner to perform a full routine and then immediately have to perform it again in front of the same audience for the benefit of the second camera. Back in the 1930s and 40s, the king of the on-camera dance routine was legendary choreographer Busby Berkeley. It has often been pointed out that many of the intricate patterns made by the overhead cameras, and supposedly part of live shows, would have made absolutely no sense to the front row of the audience who were watching them straight-on. As far as television audiences go, most of them have come along for the experience and for autographs, and are well aware that much of what goes on is for the benefit of the camera rather than for them. Nevertheless, the skills to create a good television dance piece are somewhat different from those needed to produce one live, and there are particular choreographers who specialise in this kind of dance work. If TV work is your ambition, it makes sense to find out who these choreographers are (make a note of the credit at the end of the show), and to contact them.

If you manage to get work with them, the best way to make sure they remember you for their next show is to listen carefully to instructions and make sure you stay inside your 'marks' (the lines of tape on the studio floor which show that you are within camera range). Just like everybody else in TV, such chore-ographers will be under pressure to deliver their part of the show on time and under budget.

Cruise work

If you want to be part of the classic days of light-entertainment dance shows, you can still do so – it's just that you may have to travel a little to fulfil your dreams. Cruise holidays are rivalling tribute bands as one of the growth industries of the modern showbusiness world.

In essence, the customer buys a few weeks aboard a luxury ship, the principle function of which is not so much to get them from place to place as to act as a floating pleasure city where they can relax, unwind and be entertained. From casinos to five-star restaurants, every luxury is available for those who can afford to pay – including live entertainment, which is where you come in. While there are niche cruises for newly weds and other specialised markets, the single biggest cruise audience seems to be retired couples, so a working knowledge of 1960s and 1970s music is an advantage.

Obviously cruise work is not ideally suited to dancers who don't like being cooped up and get homesick easily, but if you have no ties and want to be paid to enjoy holiday weather, cruise work is an option well worth looking into. The nature of dance is such that it lends itself very well to cruise-ship entertainment, since it is primarily visual and so suits what can be a very cosmo-politan audience. And while the five-star treatment is reserved for paying customers, most cruise performers report that the living conditions on board are very good. However, do be care-ful that you are only signing up for dance work: it is not unknown for some of the smaller cruise companies to expect performers to double up as waiters and cabin crew when they're not performing!

Showdancing

Although one of the most common images of a working dancer is the 'showgirl', most large-scale productions also feature male dancers. Places like the Las Vegas strip or the hotels and casinos of Monaco put on the showgirl type of production at its biggest and glitziest, but productions closer to home like to employ dancers who are good at this kind of work too, to recreate the glamour and glitz of such locations without quite the same budgets.

The essence of this kind of dancing is glamour, of course, so if you don't have the classic tall, long-limbed, elegant figure you are probably better off auditioning elsewhere. You also need to be confident enough to carry off the costumes. While it is not always true that these kind of dancers are called 'showgirls' because the more they show, the more they get paid, it is a fact that many of the costumes can consist more of body paint than actual fabric. From huge feather headdresses to diamante bikinis, a showdancer's main function is to dazzle (and if you're a male dancer, don't think that you won't be dressed up just as strikingly).

Probably the classic showgirl routine is the highly choreographed kick-line, sometimes with up to a hundred dancers moving in complete precision. Very impressive to watch … and very painful on the muscles if you're not used to doing it eight shows a week. For this reason many of the dancers who sparkle as showgirls and guys have solid classical dance backgrounds, and may well be doing this kind of work to support more artistic but less immediately lucrative dance ambitions.

One note of caution: because of the focus on glamour and brief costumes, the line between working as a showgirl and working as a lap dancer or stripper can get a little blurred – particularly when it comes to the way in which the jobs are described in the recruitment ads. Be sure you know what you're getting into before you commit to work that you may not want to do. We'll be looking at the 'x-rated' dance market shortly, to help you spot the distinctions and make the call.

Advertising and promotional work

As the advertising and PR industries become increasingly linked to the worlds of celebrity and showbusiness, dancers are increasingly employed to add energy, poise and colour to promotions for everything from sports clothes to breakfast cereals. Like music videos, the average TV ad campaign can have a bigger budget then several TV shows and the occasional movie put together.

If you are involved in a TV ad shoot, you will need the same skills and qualities that we have discussed in the section above. Be flexible, open to new challenges, and confident ... and bear in mind that you are just as likely to be dressed as a giant furry panda as you are a gangsta rapper. If you are involved in live promotions you may find yourself doing catwalk work in front of thousands at large trade exhibitions in Earl's Court Exhibition Centre ... and then on the next day, performing a pop routine in a shopping centre to launch a new line of crisps.

Musicals

In terms of 'making it in showbiz', appearing in a West End musical is a serious ambition for many dancers. However, while a West End run is certainly a good thing to have on your CV, there is a lot of hard work involved in such a job – and the financial rewards are not as high as you might be led to believe. The same applies for the touring versions of the hit shows. You will certainly be bringing glamour to small towns, but if you are in any way a 'home bird' you may find that one hotel starts to look pretty much the same as another after a very short time.

Despite such downsides, for many people – dancers and audiences alike – musicals are what dance is all about, and if you can sing too, this may well be where you make your name. Of course it goes without saying that singing and dancing at the same time can take a lot out of you, and this is particularly true of the current trend for 'musicals' which are in fact strings of popular songs held together by only the thinnest of plot-lines. Shows like *Smokey Joe's Café* or *Oh! What a Night!* are strenuous enough to do nightly – so by the time you have also done two matinées a week as well, you will understand why many musical cast members rarely get up before midday!

Significantly, productions where the show itself is the star, rather than any one individual 'name', often lend themselves best to touring – shows like *Boogie Nights*, or *Cats*. For these, the producer can chop and change the lead roles to keep the show fresh as it tours. Such productions can be on the road for more than five years, starting off by touring the UK and then going overseas and doing the European circuit. Occasionally, specially adapted versions have been staged on cruise ships. By the time all that overseas touring is finished, the show is often ready to start a home-tour all over again, playing to a whole new audience (or even to the same one, since these 'party' type shows tend to develop their own loyal fan following).

The plus side of all this, of course, is that if you are a versatile dancer with a lot of stamina, word can quickly spread among show producers. Just as in the music business some of the performers who work most regularly and earn most consistently are the session musicians rather than the 'named stars', so strong dancers who can keep a show's energy up can find themselves moving from job to job with very few gaps in between. And if such a dancer can sing or act a little, they often move into a lead role when the show moves from the big-city stage to the touring circuit. Then, a hard-working cast becomes more important than big names on the bill. Even if you stay in the chorus, it is not uncommon for dancers to move from one party musical to another and then back to the first one – after all, a choreographer who is brushing up an existing show for a new tour will find life easier if some of the cast already know the characters and steps.

If you are particularly good at learning songs, dialogue and steps, and have good versatile singing and dancing abilities, you may be asked to understudy a star part in a theatrical production. While this can potentially be a little frustrating if you don't have your own part in the show – all those endless rehearsals and preparations 'for nothing' – it pays dividends if you finally get to step into the role. (This doesn't always have to be because the lead is ill or in difficulties; they may just want a night off.) Famously, some understudies have ended up taking over the lead roles when the stars move on, and there are even understudies who have become stars in their own right.

Pantomimes and summer seasons

For most of the profession (including more stars than you might think!), life in showbusiness is an up-and-down process of getting the work, doing the work ... and sometimes waiting quite a long time for more work to turn up. But twice-yearly there is slightly more work around than usual, up and down the country: during the Christmas and summer holiday periods.

Although they take place at different times of the year, pantomime work and summer seasons are very similar in many regards (and not just in that they provide a welcome period of regular employment). Both are part of a very long tradition and both are firmly rooted in the entertainment rather than in the artistic side of the dance medium. Definitely not the right work environment for prima donnas, if you are a team player with a cheery personality this could well be a good annual earner for you. Pantomimes and summer seasons are cast long in advance of the actual performance dates, and the best and easiest-to-work-with performers tend to get snapped up very quickly.

In 'panto' in particular, a lively audience is more desirable than a passive one, and there is certainly a good chance that while you will get to display your regular dance skills as part of the resident troupe, you may also be involved in some comedy and slapstick sequences as a well-known comic or soap star joins in the dancing as part of their party piece. Good news for you, as you can add something interesting to your CV; and even better if the show is filmed and you can include it in your showreel.

As the name suggests, summer season work is when you join a dance troupe for one of the variety shows put on by theatres in the country's most popular seaside resorts. Like panto, these shows are designed to appeal to as wide an audience as possible, so dance routines will tend to be created around either popular songs of the last three decades, good-time musicals like *Grease*, or whatever chart hits have made an impact in the summer months. As with panto, the skills for getting booked for next year's summer season include a lot of energy, team spirit and the ability to make the named stars look good when they join in with the dance routines. The ability to live beside the sea for eight weeks and not destroy your fitness programme by living on candy floss, beer and chips, helps.

A first cousin to summer season work is working as a *Hi-Di-Hi!* style entertainer at a holiday camp. While you will have other duties besides dancing, this can be a very good grounding, both in performing and also in being part of an entertainment troupe. As former Pontins Bluecoats like Shane Richie have shown, it can also be the springboard to an established show-business career.

Ethnic dancing

Not so long ago, ethnic dancing such as Irish dancing or belly dancing was either a novelty act in family entertainment or an exotic addition to more adult-orientated shows. Shows like *Riverdance*, *Umoja* and *Bollywood Dreams* have changed all that. If you have an ethnic background and kept up those classes your parents dragged you to when you were a kid, you could well be in a very good position to reap the benefits. Not only are ethnic themed shows selling out all over the world in their own right, but there are now several ethnic dance superstars such as Michael Flatley and Joaquin Cortez. Later in the book we'll look at how one such ethnic-orientated dancer, Honey Kalaria, has expanded her activities far beyond the boundaries of her own dance style and even dance itself into a successful multi-faceted business.

Besides your own growth as a performer, honing your ethnic dance skills can get you moving in very A-list circles, as video producers constantly look for new visual angles for their latest projects. An ethnic dance specialist never knows when they may be whisked from teaching beginners at the local dance studio to being employed to teach stars like J.Lo or Janet Jackson global steps from Asian dance to Flamenco to promote their latest track.

Gospel/liturgical dance

Just as older dance traditions are becoming fashionable again, so church outreach groups are exploring ways in which to present the message of Jesus that are more relevant to modern culture. (After all, the message in its original form – storytelling – was exactly right for the time in which it was first delivered.) If your idea of gospel or church dancing is something sedate performed in flowing robes, a look at some of the dance movements currently developing in this field may change your mind.

Realistically, at least in the UK, there is still not a huge living to be made from exploring the spiritual side of your dancing. However, in terms of getting practice in expressing profound ideas through the dance medium, joining or starting a dance project in your local place of worship can be an extremely good grounding for developing dance projects in your secular career. This is one of the ways in which Jenny developed her choreography and teaching skills, leading to early experience of concert-style dance performances with top US gospel artists.

Major US gospel singers like Nicole C Mullen make dance an integral part of their concert programmes, sometimes combining it with youth work. If you are still in the youth category it may be worth finding out if any of your local churches are running dance projects. Sometimes you will find established dancers teaching as part of their church involvement at a level that would normally be far more expensive – even if they could fit it into their schedules.

Podium dancing

If you fancy attracting the attention of hundreds of people relatively early in your dance career, podium dancing may well appeal to you. Strictly speaking the attention won't solely be on you: you are as much a part of the atmosphere of a nightclub as the spotlights and dry ice, and as the name suggests you may well find yourself on top of a podium or suspended in a cage, high above the dance floor.

Basically the podium dancer's job is two-fold. First, your mission is to dress in a striking way and dance in a striking style to add to the excitement and energy of a club or pub. Second, you are there to inspire the audience members to try out their own moves and perhaps emulate the things you are doing.

Besides the money you earn, podium dancing certainly gives you a good workout. The best podium dancers have very large memory banks stuffed full of dance moves to go with every style and period of music. Just as a DJ blends together different sounds to whip the crowd into a frenzy, so a good podium dancer will combine a wide range of moves into a freestyle routine that suits the music being played – with one eye on demonstrating moves that even the most flatfooted of punters can copy, and the other on pulling the occasional move that will make for a collective 'wow' and raise the excitement level in the venue several more notches.

It stands to reason that podium dancing is best suited to more extrovert personalities (and claustrophobia or fear of heights may be a bit of a liability). It is probably something that the serious dancer would do as a fun, physical way to earn extra income rather than as a full-time career. But it is certainly compatible with a successful dance career – which is more than can be said for some of the jobs in our next category ...

Table dancing, pole dancing and lap dancing

Since this is a book about making money from dancing, it would be dishonest of us not to mention the various forms of 'dirty dancing' that can and do earn money. Whether they involve much in the way of dancing skills is more open to question. There have always been striptease- and burlesque-type establishments where one's dancing ability is secondary to the ability to take off one's clothes (not exactly rocket science). In the days when strict laws applied to exactly how much flesh could be shown, there was at least some imagination and wit involved. However, in recent years big business has taken over, so that while almost anything goes on stage, even the most *risque* show is less shocking then the fact that so many people are prepared to part with large amounts of money for titillation.

While 'sexy' dance troupes like the Chippendales have been standard hen-party fodder for several decades, the success of the *Full Monty* movie spawned a whole new range of male dance troupes of varying degrees of sophistication. And it seems like centuries ago (well, it was last century, after all) that groups like Hot Gossip steamed up our TV screens with their suggestive routines. In those days music video was still in its infancy, so TV shows were badly in need of suggestions – after all, they didn't have any visuals to accompany a record. In retrospect of course, the 'shocking' dance routines of yesteryear have quickly become tame compared to what is common on primetime TV today. Then again, in the 1920s, dances like the Charleston and the Shimmy were banned from dance halls for being too far 'over the top'.

As we have already noted, in recent times dance has become much more an integral part of the music industry, so that the likes of Christina Aguilera or Beyonce can 'shake their own booty' with the best of them. As a result the anonymous sexy dance troupe has become a bit of a dinosaur, and in its place have grown up lap-dancing, pole-dancing and table-dancing chains in the major cities – often in the financial districts. (The performers in these clubs are mainly female, for obvious reasons, but there have recently been some trials with male dancers on ladies-only nights.)

As the name suggests, dancers have to dance on a table or around a pole for the benefit of small groups of (usually drunk) clients. The dancer is usually expected to be topless at least, and the preferred dance moves are of a pretty obvious sort. The idea is to get the punter excited enough to keep spending exorbitant amounts of money on champagne and other extravagances. In the more respectable clubs, the customer is not allowed to have any contact with the dancer, except to pay for each dance. The key factor to bear in mind is that regardless of how plush the club may look, they frequently operate on a 'barber shop' system – in other words, they don't pay you to dance at their venue; *you* pay the club to be allowed to dance. The club takes a percentage of your earnings and you keep the rest.

And in some clubs your 'duties' may go a lot further than dancing. While it would be an exaggeration to say that outright prostitution is involved, you may be expected to sit with clients and generally flatter and coax them into spending as much money as possible while they are at the venue. The potential dangers of this kind of activity are obvious – but more to the point, if you have any kind of vision of a serious dance career, you need to consider properly whether this kind of work is something you are going to want people to know about in the future. If you do decide to go ahead at this kind of club, insist at the very least that you have a contract and that everything you are agreeing to do – and more important, what you do *not* consent to do – is included in the terms of the contract.

There have indeed been some mainstream dancers, actresses and singers who started off in the so-called glamour market and made good. It is just that we know of a lot more who intended to do this just to get themselves started in the business, and ended up cynical, sold-out and cast aside once their looks and marketability faded. 'Easy money' doesn't seem so easy when it costs you your future dreams.

Modelling, magic, monsters, etc.

Since dancers by their nature are people who know how to use their bodies and also (hopefully) take time to keep those bodies fit and looking good, they are often suited to working in areas which, while not strictly dance-related, can be interesting, fun and pay good money. An obvious example is modelling: indeed, while some dancers supplement their income with modelling jobs, many go the whole hog and list themselves as 'model/dancer' or 'dancer/model' on their CVs and in their promotional materials. Bear in mind that modelling doesn't necessarily have to be full-figure; if you have particularly long legs or the right kind of hands, close-up shots for tights or jewellery may well become a good source of income for you. Remember to read adverts for models carefully to distinguish genuine jobs from the sleaze merchants. Be aware, too, that if you are looking for inter-national work, in some parts of the US the word 'dancer' can be taken to mean lap dancer or stripper – so you will need to establish clearly what the jobs you are applying for involve and what you are prepared, or not prepared, to do.

Some other showbusiness roles, such as a magician's assis-tant, also lend themselves well to physiques which are both attractive and flexible (for squeezing into secret compartments) and can be a good source of extra income. But these days it is computer artists who work the real magic, creating whole new worlds for video games or special-effects movies populated with weird and wonderful creatures. In order to bring these creations to life, the computer images are often modelled on the move-ments of real-life people captured on special cameras. Dancers are used to both physical performance and taking instructions, so they are ideal models for computer artists to work with. A day or two spent covered in sensor pads can result in a very attractive wage packet and a starring role as an alien warrior from Planet ZZurg!

The above examples are of course just the tip of the iceberg in terms of the unusual jobs that a creatively minded dancer – or a dancer who just happens to be at the right casting at the right time – can end up doing. And of course, you can always create your own work ...

Your own show

Creating your own work may well be the opposite of 'easy money', but it can be very rewarding. If you are really serious about dance, there will come a time when you decide to move away from interpreting other people's ideas and start to express your own. How you develop the artistic side of that expression is a little outside the scope of this career-based book, although in the resource section you will find several recommendations for books which will help you develop your ideas. But from a purely commercial perspective, putting together your own dance show can have a two-fold benefit. First of all, it gives you something to focus on between jobs, and a potential showcase for your work to which you can invite suitable people as part of your personal marketing campaign (see also Chapter Three). Second, in a profession where most people spend their time waiting for someone else to provide the work, developing your one-person show means that you have a 'product' with which you can potentially earn money independently – if you are prepared to put some initial effort into designing, producing and marketing it.

Obviously, if you are focusing in any way on the commercial possibilities of a show, it may be best to base it on some theme which is of interest or accessible to the general audience, rather than just to the dance connoisseur. 'Themed' shows lend themselves especially well to arts festivals, where pre-existing programme slots are often available, together with a requirement to include dance alongside other art forms like drama and music. If your dance piece draws its inspiration from another art form such as a favourite author or playwright, literary festivals may also be interested in you as a break from straight readings.

Since festival slots tend to be between 45 minutes and one hour, it makes sense for your show to run for a similar length of time. However, that is an extremely long time to spend on stage without a lot of creativity and imagination. For this reason a number of dancers may decide to come together to put on a show. This can certainly lead to an end product which is more successful artistically than any of them could have achieved working independently; but of course, it can only work if all parties involved agree on a shared vision – not to mention shared billing.

A special show is certainly a good way to make a name for yourself in the dance world, but for that reason you also need to be sure that you make it a good show. If this is a part of your vision, even in the distant future, you should make a habit of seeking out as many one-person shows as you can to see what you like and don't like, what you can learn and what you would do better given the chance. Additionally, since your own show may also involve you as producer, director, choreographer, stage manager and marketing executive, it will be useful for you to observe as many experts in these fields at work as you possibly can. The best way to do that is to get some work yourself in a variety of professional dance productions and environments.

We hope that this chapter has given you some idea of just how varied dance work can be. In the next, we will look at how you go about ensuring that some of that work comes your way. But before we do, here is Jenny's own career story, showing how a variety of early experiences can start to add up.

I was one of those kids who was always running around, exerting so much energy that my mum would shout at me to 'stop prancing around the house'. I was a real tomboy, not interested in boys or playing kiss-chase (yuk!). Give me marbles and I would sit at a drain, put on a record and dance my little heart out – yet there was no intention on my part to become a dancer!

At school I always took part in games and anything that had to do with dance. I used to watch Ben Vereen or Gregory Hines, amongst others, gliding across the floor with such style that it was effortless; every little movement was inspirational. Anyway, one day my mother decided to send me to ballet classes. Inside my head this little voice said 'Ugh ... too girlie, all frills and silly little girls in pink tutus and ballet shoes', and boy, was I miserable. But I went along and after a while really enjoyed it, receiving honours on passing my exams. Although there was some bullying towards me because of it, being the loud person that I am I handled the situation rather well.

At the age of 16 I found myself in an African dance company called Black Tulip. This was after having had a break from dancing for four years, after our teacher retired

– just as we were about to start working on blocks! The company was really exciting and different from anything else I'd previously experienced. When it came to a close, it was sad: dancing wasn't high on my agenda, so I didn't dance again until 1994, when I met Sam Crosby who taught dance at a modelling agency where I taught deportment.

Sam taught at Danceworks and he invited me to his classes. That was it – hooked again, still not realising that my calling was calling me! After a few years of dancing with Sam there was no challenge for me, no one to feed off, to push me further with my ability. During that period of my life I had two close friends and we used to hang out all the time, getting noticed by other dancers and being challenged by the guys (they always feel threatened when they see a girl that can dance just as well as they can!). This path led me to perform for Aaron Hall and Tim Westwood. Amongst other work I appeared in All Saints' first videos. The friendship died down after a while and I changed classes at Danceworks.

After that I started attending classes taught by Dennis Wonder, as a beginner. There was no way on earth that I was going to start at intermediate level; my biggest mistake was to watch that lesson before mine started, and this little voice in my head was telling me, 'You're going to look silly, you can't do it.' So foolishly, I stayed in my comfort zone as a beginner. This went on for at least six months, as Dennis kept telling me to try intermediate and I kept saying, 'Yeah, maybe next week,' but next week never came. Until one session, when one of the students turned to me and asked me why I was doing that particular level when I should be in intermediate. On hearing that, Dennis turned round and told me, 'I want to see you in intermediate next week.' He wasn't asking me, he was telling me … I felt like strangling the student who had spoken out!

The following week there was no choice, it had to be done, bite the bullet and throw yourself into it. Boy, did I get kicked and knocked … believe me, I wanted to tear someone's head off, the humiliation was unbearable and I could see myself leaving the class. Knowing how Dennis is, though, he would have called me back in front of everyone, and that thought made me more determined to try. But there was still that sense of doubt – of not being good enough, always staying in the back so no one could see me making mistakes.

In 2002 I stopped going to classes due to the lack of confidence which had built up over a period of time. No matter how much someone told me that 'I was an excellent dancer', I didn't believe them. (The devil is very good at playing tricks with you at your most vulnerable stage.) Cleansing is very good for the soul, and taking time out then was the best thing I could have done – stepping back, taking a look at my life and seeing where it was going. I realised that I was gradually turning into all the other girls that came to class and starting to lose my own identity. In saying that, I'm really grateful to Dennis. He gave me so much advice over the years, with tips on clothing, hair, the kind of style directors are looking for, always correcting me. More than that, he has also been a good friend, and still is; if it wasn't for his teaching methods I wouldn't have gone back into dance.

It was strange going back after a year's break, but I knew in my heart of hearts that the time was right. My head was clear from all the doubt and lack of confidence. There was no stopping the passion that was in me, and I came to realise that deep down, dancing has always been what I wanted to do. It didn't matter any more that I wasn't chosen at auditions or that my image wasn't quite what they were looking for, as long as I was dancing – that's the only thing that matters to me. Sharing that with other people, and talking about my experiences, has also helped me come to terms with who I am.

One thing I always say to dancers is: 'Don't let age stop you from succeeding or from following a career in dance.' Many a time there have been comments made and questions asked about my own age, with the occasional sly remark, but I think of it this way – what does that person see in you that scares them in order for them to try and put you off?

This chapter of my life has been the best yet, and it can only get better. Never give up and be strong, follow your heart and have faith in your own ability.

Jenny's story is proof that whatever stage your dance career is at – whether you're a beginner or someone who has put their career 'on hold' – it is never too late to start, or to start moving forwards again. And now let's move forwards too – to the chapter which aims to help you kick-start *your* success story.

Chapter Three

Best Foot Forwards ...

Marketing for the working dancer

If we were to ask you to name your favourite dancer, who would that be? Someone you saw on stage or on TV when you were very young – the person who first ignited your desire to forge your own career as a dancer? Perhaps it would be one of the dance legends like Nijinsky or Josephine Baker who continue to inspire generations, or a teacher you studied with as part of your dance training – someone with not just their own tremendous dance talent, but also the equally important gift of being able to use their own passion to touch, move and motivate others. It could even be Jenny Belingy (if it's John, you must be very keen on novelty dance acts).

We are asking the question for two reasons: first because it is important to have a role model; but also because in the context of this chapter, we want to point up a difference between dance and some of the other popular art forms. If you were primarily a singer or an actor and told us who had most influenced you, there would be a better-than-average chance that we would be familiar with the name. If the person you named was in the first category – someone excellent at their craft but not quite a legend, or someone who has chosen the relative anonymity of teaching – we would nod our heads in recognition, even if we weren't completely familiar with that person's work. Even if the singer you mentioned was a one-hit wonder, or if the actor was in one reasonably successful movie, it's possible that a sizeable proportion of the general public would recall hearing the song or seeing the film – at least vaguely.

With dance it is different: a dancer may be highly respected within the profession, but almost unknown to the outside world. Dancers who have made the breakthrough into celebrity status tend to have done so by adding other strings to their bow – like

Paula Abdul, for example, who is a very accomplished choreographer behind the scenes but came to public attention as a singer with two hit albums, and latterly as a foil to Simon 'Mr Nasty' Cowell on *American Idol*.

There are a number of understandable reasons why individual dancers don't get their name above the title as some fellow performers do. For one thing, the nature of commercial dance is such that you will quite often be in the background or part of a support act for singers or presenters. As we noted in the last chapter, the ability to blend into a team is sometimes more important in the dance world than the ability to stand out. While the individual strengths of each dancer are what make a dance troupe or dance production great, it is usually the troupe or the production itself which is the 'star'.

However, while this may make artistic sense (whether or not it makes sense to your ego), it certainly doesn't mean that dancers shouldn't pay attention to the marketing side of their career. This is not just because our world is increasingly obsessed with image and branding; it is more fundamentally because as a dancer, you are in effect a self-employed business person. Businesses which wait for their customers to find them rather than keeping themselves in the forefront of their customers' minds are liable to sink rather than swim.

If you are like many performers, the word 'marketing' may well make you wince – after all, you got into the dance business to dance. Most dancers are perfectly happy to sign up with an agent or preferably a number of agencies and leave the marketing to them. We can understand that, and later on in this chapter we'll talk about what to look for in an agent ... and what to watch out for in agents you shouldn't let near you with a ten-foot pole! However, we firmly believe that not only is every performer a business in their own right, but also that they must get used to acting as the managing director of that business. As their career progresses they may well bring other people on board to take care of some of the aspects of their career they have no time for, or just aren't all that gifted at. But as any successful managing director will tell you, you can't get someone to do something for you if you don't know what that 'something' is – and you can't check that they are doing it properly if you haven't at least had a go at it yourself.

With this in mind we are going to talk first about how you can best market yourself. After all, even if you decide to rely totally on agents, you will first have to market yourself to those agents to get them to represent you. Ask any performer who is not getting as much work as they would like what they would want an agent to do for them, and the first thing they will usually say is: 'Get me in front of the right people.' A good agent will certainly have a list of the best contacts for getting his or her clients work – but that list wasn't built up by magic. As soon as you set foot outside your front door, you are making contacts too. The secret of turning those contacts into work is to make sure that you collect them somewhere and keep them safe, and that you know what to do with them.

Your mailing list

Open any CD case, log onto any performer's website, buy a branded pair of dance shoes and the chances are that you'll be asked for your name or address. You may also be asked about your occupation, background and income, and you may even get a free gear bag thrown in – but what the people behind the CDs, websites and shoes want most of all is your precious name and address, so they can build up a mailing list, contact you again, and lead you to other products that you'll be interested in buying. You need to do the same.

We usually recommend that performers keep two mailing lists. The first one is for your 'fan base' – the people who you know for sure like what you are doing. They are your customers, and they are a very important part of your business. You should aim to be growing this list throughout your career: if you haven't been doing so already, today is as good a day as any to start. Grab a sheet of paper, or better yet a computer keyboard, and start to list the name, address and contact details of everyone who's ever come to your gigs, encouraged you to keep dancing or expressed interest in any aspect of your work. If this hasn't been something you've bothered about up until now, you may find some of the missing information in old diaries and on torn-up bits of paper. Some of it will probably be gone forever. Don't worry about it – simply make it a habit from now on to never let one of those people get away without getting contact details for them.

For now you can simply collect this information in a note-book, or if you have a website (see pp. 54–5) you can set up a simple pop-up form for the purpose. If someone comes up after a gig to tell you that they enjoyed what you did, simply ask for their name and address 'so I can let you know about my next gig'. If they genuinely enjoyed your show they should be happy to sign up. And why should you knock yourself out 'cold selling' each new gig or project to new people when you have an existing group of admirers who are already sold on your work?

Mailing list number two is a list of all the people *in the entertainment industry* who can give you the chance to make new fans. You can't reach your audience unless you have venues to perform in, shows to be part of and spotlights to stand in, so you need to be selling yourself to everyone in the entertainment world who can provide those things. You'll also find it a lot easier to persuade those people to use you if they know how great your usual work is – so another section of your list will include publications and journalists you would like to review your work. And if you want to share your talent with a wider audience, then TV producers and casting agents need to be in your sights. Just having their names on your list won't guarantee you their attention, of course – but *not* letting them know what you can do will pretty much ensure that your light remains under a bushel.

Your two lists – of fan base and professional contacts – are related. Producers need to put bums on seats, and to entertain them while they're there; journalists need to bump up circulation figures with articles about star performers; and TV producers are always looking to harvest the best of acts that have proven to be both successful and popular live. If you can prove that you've got a big enough fan base, you're a long way along the road to getting these people to take you seriously.

Market research

Ask most aspiring dancers whom they want their art to appeal to, and the usual answer is 'everybody'. It's certainly true that the best entertainers can appeal to every sort of audience regardless of age, gender or musical preference ... but when you've got a limited marketing budget and an even more limited marketing 'team' (possibly just you in your spare time), 'everybody' is a rather big market to be aiming for. To get the best return on your efforts you need to focus them efficiently.

Although dance is a creative art form, in the marketing context it is helpful to think of it simply as a product you are selling. Like everyone else who has a product to sell, one of the most useful ways to focus your efforts is to take some time to work out exactly who your primary audience is. These are the people who are likely to pick up on what you are doing and give you the biggest fan base in the shortest space of time. Sometimes there can be a particular audience that you really want to reach: for many dancers this is their own peer-group audience, be they teenagers or '30 somethings'. Other entertainers go for a different market, which, though smaller, can often be easier to conquer. For example, dance groups such as the Jiving Lindy Hoppers have revived swing dance from the 1930s and 40s and made this into a multifaceted business ranging from exciting stage shows to classes for students aged nine to 90.

Once you have identified your target audience, you then need to think about their likes and dislikes. Where do they go for entertainment? What TV and radio shows do they watch? Which venues do they go to to see their favourite musicals and dance shows? You need to start visiting those venues, watching those programmes and subscribing to the newsletters of those theatres – and not just for entertainment purposes. Try really hard to identify common elements in delivery, packaging or subject matter which make these particular performers or productions appeal to the target audience. You've now begun your market research.

The next step is to attract the attention of the right people – i.e. those who can bring you in front of your chosen market. The director of a specific dance company? The choreographer of a certain show, or an influential journalist whose column everybody in the dance world reads? These are your mailing-list people – but you can't put them on the list until you find out who they are.

Contacts

The reason many aspiring dancers (and many more experienced ones) give for not being able to reach that elusive audience of 'everybody' is that they 'just don't have the contacts'. It's true that if you could just pick up the phone and call the right people, things might move a lot quicker. However, even if you're not yet on first-name terms with them, you can certainly improve your chances of getting your name in front of the right people by researching who the right people actually are.

Keep an eye on the dance press: lots of titles are listed in the resource section at the end of this book. Search the Internet, pick up the phone, dial the company switchboard and ask. Whether it's the programme manager of your local theatre or the arts development officer of your local council, once you've got their specific name and title you have someone to direct your marketing at. But what do you send them?

Marketing materials

In these highly visual times, your image as a dancer is as important as your dance skills themselves. Marketing and business communications are an important part of this image: in fact, as they are quite often the *first* contact someone will have with you, this is one of the most vital areas to get right.

At the beginning of your career in particular, you may not have a huge (or even any) marketing budget. Even so, try to make the best of what you do have through neatness, professionalism and attention to detail. If your budget stretches to having your own letterhead, wonderful; even better if you can persuade a design-minded friend to come up with a 'logo' for you. But at the very least make sure that every piece of print that has your name on it is clean, clear and on good-quality paper. It's hardly going to persuade anyone that you are a stylish, experienced act if the letter telling them so is crumpled, handwritten and accompanied by a grainy second-generation photocopy of a six-year-old photograph.

Whether or not you can afford to get a professional letterhead designed, we would certainly encourage you to get a decent set of business cards as soon as you start out. Business cards are small enough to carry with you when you are performing, so that when someone approaches you after a show to (hopefully) offer you more work you can give them your contact details easily instead of scrabbling around for a biro and the back of a cigarette packet. Cards are also great to have on hand when unexpected marketing opportunities arise: you never know whom you may come into contact with in the course of your day job or at a social occasion – perhaps they have need of a dancer, or contacts in the music or entertainment industries.

Although your budget may be tight, try to make sure that the card you hand over isn't one of the mass-produced ones obtained from vending machines. If you're an original, the information you give to people should be, too. And aside from the impact your card will have on potential clients, there is an added benefit in the impact it will have on you. Seeing your name on a nice-looking card with the words 'professional dancer' printed underneath can really help you focus on making that dream a reality.

Right from the start, try to make your letters, biographies and any other piece of communication as polished and error-free as possible. This means checking spellings and grammar and – unless you're sending a thank-you card or short personal note – making sure that everything is typed rather than handwritten. Whether you're pitching a theatre owner to get onstage at their venue or a choreographer to gain an audition, your contact will certainly be wondering how good your performance skills are … but they'll also be influenced by more mundane concerns such as how professional you are, will you turn up on time, is it worth their giving valuable time to finding out more about you? If you can't even be bothered to make your initial communication look professional, it doesn't exactly give the impression that your attitude to dancing will be any different. If writing or typing isn't your strong suit, get someone else to help you out. As your career progresses you'll find you use the same letters and documents over and over again, from confirming gig bookings to sending out invoices, so it will save a lot of time to have your standard letters stored on computer. In that way you can customise them and send them out as and when they are needed.

Above all, use your common sense. Every time we teach marketing to performers, some of them express surprise that we take the time to offer advice on how to put a piece of paper into an envelope. Sadly, we have frequently been on the receiving end of letters and packages which a performer has obviously spent a lot of time compiling – and then crammed into an envelope which is too small or too flimsy to survive in the mail.

Test marketing

A very good way to gauge the effectiveness of your sales and marketing effort is to identify someone who works in business. Although it is nice if that person works in the dance business, or in some other branch of showbusiness, any business will do. Once you find your 'test contact', send them your promotional package *as if they have never heard of you*. Ask them to tell you honestly what impression they would form from the package alone, and if it would prompt them to pick up the phone and find out more. If not, why not? If you can manage enough detachment, you could even try sending a sample package to yourself. Just as every performer can learn a lot from 'sitting in their own audience', so putting yourself in the place of a recipient of your promotional material can identify some easily made but nonetheless fundamental oversights. A surprising number of people put together a decent promo pack – but forget to include any contact details to allow the client to get back to them.

Assuming you *have* remembered to include your contact details, what can you do to help ensure that the recipient is encouraged to use them? Getting the person's name right helps. After all, a letter is far more likely to be dealt with if it is addressed to a specific person rather than just a job title. Phone and find out the full name of the appropriate person, and be sure to check how their name is spelt. People are very sensitive about their names and titles at the best of times, and particularly so in the ego-driven world of showbusiness, so there's no surer way to annoy someone than by getting their name wrong in a letter.

Whatever the title or position of the person you're writing to, write on the assumption that they are both important and busy. Yes, you're a dancer and not an insurance broker so you don't have to be ultra-formal; but equally, letters which are too 'artistic', jokey, 'in your face' or telling your entire life story are liable to do more harm than good. Basically your initial approach should tell the reader who you are, explain what's unique or different about you, specify what you have to offer them, tell them what you've enclosed to demonstrate that you can deliver (i.e. CDs, photos, videos or a biography), and finally suggest what they might do or whom they might contact to find out more. If you have done your market research then you have already found out what a venue, company or individual is looking for in advance: your letter tells them how you are the solution to their search. More to the point, market research stops you wasting time and money pitching to the wrong targets – one of the reasons why the majority of pitches are dead in the water before the envelope is even opened.

As we have already mentioned in our previous chapters, just because you have majored in one dance discipline doesn't mean that you can't find work in other areas. However, if your background is in classical ballet, and you are looking to join a touring production of *Saturday Night Fever*, it is up to you to make the connection and point out the good reasons why your background will add an extra element to the show. Don't expect the producers to make the leap by some form of telekinesis.

Photos

Visuals are becoming the most important element of almost every branch of performance. These days even the best singers will find it hard-going in the music industry if they don't have 'the look' to go with their sound. And when record companies sign singers, they usually expect to put as much money into developing their look as they do their sound. As a working dancer, you can't wait around for someone else to develop your look – it is one of your most important selling tools. And the first time many of your potential clients are going to see you is when they receive your photo.

With this in mind, it's worth getting your photos done as soon as you can – but put both time and effort into getting them right. Because photos are such a powerful marketing tool, you're going to go through a lot of them; however, photoshoots are expensive so at the beginning of your career you'll want to get some good shots that you can go on using for some time.

This book was written so that you can dip in and out of it, trying whatever bits of advice appeal to you, keeping what works and discarding the rest. But there is one piece of advice that we'd ask you to take at face value: *get your photographs taken by a professional photographer* – and preferably one who is used to taking shots of performers. It doesn't matter how good a photographer your best friend is, or how hi-tech your camera; 'homemade' photos instantly mark you out as an amateur. (Passport photos, graduation photos and masterpieces by the local wedding photographer count as 'homemade' for these purposes too.)

To find a good photographer, ask another performer who has good photos to put you in contact with the person who took them. If you don't know anyone with good pictures, trade papers like *The Stage* run small ads by many specialist photographers plying for trade (but make sure you don't confuse the ads for portrait photographers with the ads for photographers seeking 'glamour models').

Whether or not a particular photographer has been recommended to you, ask to see examples of their work. Just like dancers, each photographer has their own individual style, and it's worth shopping around to find one that suits you. Bear in mind that it is not the photographer's job to create your 'image' for you – that's something you should have worked out in advance. What you are looking for is someone who can capture that image and show it off to best advantage. Ideally you should be aiming to build up a good portfolio of shots – say, one good head-and-shoulders photo and a number of striking body shots showing you in different dance modes and costumes. If at the beginning of your career cash is really tight, just go for a good-quality head-and-shoulders shot. As long as your vital statistics are listed on your CV, clients should be able to work out from this whether or not they are interested in calling you for an interview.

These days, computer technology allows even the smallest studio to 'improve' photos. By all means have the odd blemish removed if the service is offered, but do make sure that you still look like the photo or you'll defeat the whole purpose of including it in your pack. On this note, unless you have the means to get new shots taken regularly, you'll have to be wary of making radical changes to your image – such as getting very long hair cropped short – if you want your photos to remain current.

It goes without saying that a good photographer should put you at your ease and listen to your ideas, even if they have better ones based on their own experience. On the other hand, if the photographer doesn't seem particularly bothered or interested in what you want to achieve, you are probably better off looking elsewhere. It's usually a good idea to check out a couple of photographers price-wise before making a final decision. More expensive doesn't necessarily mean better quality. In times gone by, good-quality black-and-white photos were the best choice of the cash-strapped beginner, for economic reasons. These days black-and-white film costs as much if not more than colour, but monochrome photos are still the most versatile. They can be reproduced in all kinds of media and, taken properly, can look very 'classy'. By all means get good colour shots done too – but even when you've got them, make sure they also look good when reproduced in black-and-white as they might appear in a newspaper article or on a flyer.

In general, the more photos you order, the less the cost of each one. So, assuming that you've got a good-quality photo to start with, get as many done as possible so that you've got a good supply available. Again, while the classic 8 x 10 shots are very nice, postcard-sized is a lot more versatile and economic if the paying work hasn't started rolling in just yet.

How does one achieve photos that might lead to paying work? A little preparation before the session helps. For a start, try to book the session for a time when you can get there easily and in good form: arriving late and sweaty from a crowded bus won't help to create a glamorous image. Your photo should look reasonably close to the image that you present on stage, but you should also spend some time identifying your best or most striking physical features (it helps to get an objective opinion from people whom you trust). These are the features you may want to emphasise in the photos, pointing them up by the pose you adopt or perhaps the lighting that you use. That's the photographer's job, and another good reason why it's important to choose an experienced one.

Bring along dance gear that makes you feel confident and looking at your best, and allow yourself time to change into it. It may or may not help the photographer to have a tape of the kind of music that best sums up your dance style, or a visual image of you in performance – but even if it just helps *you*, feel free to bring those things along. Remember that ultimately, you are the only one who knows what image you want to put across. It's worth persevering until you get it.

Actors are often advised to wear little if any make-up for their photos, to allow their 'natural' selves to shine through.

Slightly different advice may be appropriate for a dancer, particularly if their stage persona is glamorous or sophisticated. A good photographer should be able to adjust the lighting to best effect even if you are just wearing normal make-up, but if you have make-up people or stylists as part of your support team it's a good idea to get them involved – or at least to get their advice before the session, always bearing in mind that *professional* advice and experience should be what you are after, not interference from well-meaning friends.

In her book *High Kicks*, experienced dancer and choreographer Donna Ross makes the very sensible suggestion that you bring along a dancer friend whom you trust to the photoshoot. They can cast their eye over whatever poses you adopt and tell you if your tummy is sticking out! Another good reason for bringing a friend along: 'Murphy's Law' dictates that on the day of your photo session something will happen to depress you, distract you and generally make you feel like hiding your head under the bedcovers rather than showing off your talents to the world. (It's also in the nature of performers – particularly female, but also more males than may care to admit it – never to be one hundred percent happy with their physical appearance ... so the prospect of being photographed is especially likely to bring all those insecurities to the fore.) Your friend can help to cheer and encourage you, making sure that you get the best out of your session and the money you are spending on it.

However you feel on the day, treat the photo session just like you would a show, and make the camera your audience. Since you are looking for a shot that will be usable for a year or two, try to visualise where you hope to be in that time, and step into that image right now. Today you may have to walk home from the session because you can't afford the bus fare, but tomorrow you may travel in a limousine. Your dream is to dance your way to the very top of your profession; for the purposes of the photo session at least, start acting out that dream as if it's already a reality.

Your CV

Your CV is a list of all the dance jobs you have done to date. It may also include a few other jobs if they are in some way related to the job you are currently applying for. While your photos will need to last you for a reasonable period of time, you will be aiming to update your CV more often. As you get more jobs, and therefore more raw material to use on it, you will produce a specially tailored CV for each letter you send. For instance, if you are applying for work as a dancer in a panto, you may want to focus your CV on other live shows you have performed in; while if it is a music video you are targeting, then other music-orientated work is obviously most relevant.

As with your photo, although dancers' CVs tend to follow a fairly standard format (listing name, address, contact numbers, vital statistics, Equity and other relevant memberships, training and work experience to date, and any special skills you may have), you can emphasise the elements that present you in the best light. Many dancers also recommend playing down or even leaving out dates (including your date of birth) – since unfortunately, age prejudice does exist in the dance world. Simply list your most relevant work in reverse order (most recent first, moving back to your student days). If producers really want to know when a particular event happened, they can always ask.

While it is perfectly acceptable to chop and change the work you've done to suit each application, don't be tempted to exaggerate or lie about skills you have or jobs you've done. It's neither big nor clever. More to the point, the dance world is very small and you will get found out, usually when it will do the most damage to your future work prospects.

Keep your CV brief – preferably on one page of A4. If the recipient hasn't made up their mind to see you after one page, reams of further information won't change things. Another advantage of keeping your CV to one page is that as you do more work, you'll have to drop the smaller and less impressive jobs to make room, ensuring that your CV remains a list of your 'greatest hits'.

Videos/CD-ROMs/DVDs

Although a letter, photo, CV and determination are the only tools essential for marketing yourself, it can certainly help to include good-quality video clips of your performances in your marketing package, on cassette, CD-ROM or DVD. However, everything we have said about photos applies here in spades, and in particular the bits relating to quality. You may be one of the world's most exciting entertainers, able to hold an audience in the palm of your hand, but a homemade video shot in bad light from the third row of your cousin's wedding reception is hardly likely to confirm your reputation. (And please don't think we're exaggerating here – the quality of some of the videos we get sent, often from experienced performers who should know better, would honestly make you weep.)

A look at the credits of any professional concert video, shot using multiple cameras and extensive post-production and sound remixing, will confirm just how much the professionals spend on getting things right. Even then, what is sold as a 'live concert performance' is quite frequently *several* live concert performances shot on different nights with the best bits edited together to give the illusion of the perfect show. You may not be able to stump up a multi-million dollar production budget just yet, but if you are planning to use video as part of your selling package you must be prepared to invest a reasonable amount of money in proper equipment and in people who know how to operate it. You also need to be able to communicate to the video team what you are trying to achieve before you go onstage. You can't be worrying about how the video's going to turn out when you're in the spotlight trying to give a show that's worth capturing on tape.

Reviews and showreels

No matter how impressive your photos, demos and other promotional material may be, people in the dance business are often reluctant to rely on these – preferring a recommendation by someone they know and trust. This is not unusual: many medical products are sold on the back of doctors' recommendations; pet foods are promoted as the ones that 'nine out of ten owners prefer'; and a good press review – even if it's just one line long – is likely to appear on an artist's promos and posters for many years. 'A stunning performer', 'stylish, sexy, sensational', 'the next big thing' – if anyone has said anything complimentary about you in print, hang on to it and let other people know about it. It's only natural that before we invest our time or hard-earned cash in something, we like to know that someone else has been there (and liked it) before us. One or two good reviews from respected sources can make all the difference in persuading someone to book you or to spend money on a ticket to come and see you.

And yes, there are people who brazenly make up press quotes and sometimes complete reviews. That's between you and your conscience – but remember that aside from any moral issue, whatever claims you make for your act in your promotional material should be for things you can actually *deliver* on when the curtain goes up, or you will very quickly come unstuck. As for the even more common practice of taking just the best bits of a review, often out of context, and quoting them ... well, let's just say that if your posters and flyers say 'Amazing! *The Times*' when the original *Times* reviewer said, 'It's amazing that anyone this bad should actually be onstage,' it might be best if you put your promotional work aside and put in a lot more rehearsal time before anyone else comes to see you.

On a more serious note, if you do get good reviews – as an individual or for a show you have been in – make sure you get several copies of them to keep (you can usually buy back numbers from the publication's head office if you miss the news-stand edition). A good clippings selection, neatly and properly photo-copied, can look very impressive when included in your package.

You don't have to just wait and hope that the press will turn up to see you do your stuff. As long as you are confident that you can deliver the goods, why not take the bull by the horns and invite dance critics and reviewers to your forthcoming gigs? It's true that journalists, particularly the influential ones, get invited to many more events than they can actually attend. However, anyone who works in the press will tell you that they also have deadlines and empty spaces to fill on a regular basis, so it might just be that your letter or press release arrives at a time when they are stuck for inspiration. The better you get at identifying what is unique and exciting about your act, the more chance you will have of convincing the press that you are worth coming down to see.

If you're appearing in professional shows or doing special charity gigs, it may be that the venue or organisers are already doing some publicity. Most of us find, though, that the only way of guaranteeing the best possible coverage is to take the responsibility for doing it ourselves and viewing whatever marketing anyone else does as a bonus. Just as with your cover letter and other elements of your promotion, make sure that any press information you send out has your contact numbers clearly visible, as well as details of the date and time of the event. Although major journalists don't usually worry about admission fees, a line like 'Please contact me if you would like to come along and I will arrange to put you on the guest list' may attract the attention of writers from smaller publications. (Check in advance that you can do this, of course.) If you're aiming to build up a reputation in your local area, don't underestimate the power of the local press. You can also actively pitch yourself to television shows, instead of sitting around waiting for them to come and discover you. When it comes to existing or long-running shows you can find all the production details and relevant names on the end credits.

Unlike for singers or comedians (and it's not easy for them either, these days), there aren't that many slots for dancers on primetime TV – but it's not unknown for dancers to use lateral thinking to get a little screen time. For instance, there are an increasing number of 'makeover' items on daytime TV, and sometimes entire makeover channels. Applying for a makeover that will suit your dancer's image may well give you a chance to display your dance skills too, since TV producers are always looking for interesting visual ways to dress up the same old items. Going on a quiz show and mentioning that you are a dancer may get you an invitation to 'give a twirl'.

Whether you get your TV moments by 'sideways' routes like these, or actually start to build up TV dance gigs (see Chapter Four on auditions), a proper showreel will be of more benefit to you than sending out long tapes of shows that you were in for just a few seconds. Even if you only have one TV appearance under your belt, edit it down professionally so that you and your performance are the only thing on the tape.

Websites

Your own website can be a highly effective marketing tool and a great way of building up your fan base. You can include photos, biographical information and music downloads; you can even sell CDs, t-shirts and other merchandise if you have a real head for business. These days there are enough simple software packages around that even the least 'techie' dancer can use to design and construct a site that reflects their own unique image and personality with relative ease.

The resource section at the end of this book lists a number of sites, both of organisations and of individual dancers, to give you an idea of what is possible. However, the key thing to remember about websites is that the most amazing site in the world is no good if nobody actually logs on to it. Once you've got a web address, search to see if you can register your stage name or a variation of it. Then you will need to publicise your site as much as possible – and that often involves going back to old-fashioned print methods!

Agents

As we said at the beginning of this chapter, the only person who can really market you effectively is *you*. Spend time practising some or all of the above marketing methods and you'll learn not just more about marketing, but a lot more about your fan base and the elements of your act that appeal to them. When you have generated enough interest through your own efforts, to the point where some other person or company is interested in coming on board and marketing you, having done the job yourself will ensure that your career remains true to your original vision.

Having said that, for dancers more than for most other per-formers, agents and agencies are a vital source of ongoing work – especially at the beginning of a career. The truth is that while a good reputation is your best marketing tool, building that reputation takes time and requires the right jobs and environ-ments to show your stuff both on and offstage. An agent or dance agency with a good reputation already has the contacts and clients who can give you those much-needed work opportunities. In fact, many dancers work with several agencies at a time. If you have developed a good basic promotional package using our guidelines above, you can use it to promote your talents to agents just as you would to independent clients. But although it may be you who makes the initial approach to an agent, before you even look for representation there are two fundamental rules to remember. Whether they are individuals or companies:

1 **Agents are *not* your employer.** If anything, you are *their* employer in that they make their money from the work you do. Hopefully they earn that money by getting you work that you wouldn't get in the first place (that's certainly the main reason for employing one). However, even if the work does come through some other source – let's say someone has recommended you, or you have worked for the same company before and they want you back – the agent may still expect their 'cut'. To earn it, it is their job to negotiate better terms for you than you would get yourself. However the work comes to you, payment for the job will go to your agent first; you have every right to expect them to pass it on to you, less their percentage, in a reasonable time.

Most good agencies understand their role in your career and are clear about it in their contracts. But there are still far too many performers (and not all of them are beginners) who view their agent almost as a 'boss' and accept bad or even no service as if they can't do anything about it.

2 **Your agent is *not* your manager.** This is true even if it says 'manager' on their business card. As we noted above, an agent's job is to send out your details to people who may give you work, and to negotiate the best possible terms for you when they do. While a good and experienced agent can give you guidance and advice (which you should certainly listen to), the only person who can make decisions about your career is you. And in order to do this, you need to have a game plan for your career worked out before you even approach an agent. That way you can work out which one (or ones) will best help you achieve it. The big stars may have their entourages to tend to their every whim (perhaps J.Lo's notoriously large circle of managers and minders is a result of having to carry a huge dancer's bag around all by herself during her hoofing days?) – but even at that level, there is no doubting the fact that it is the performer themselves who is the captain of their career ship.

And now that you have got those two facts clear in your head, you are ready to sail into the choppy waters of agent-hunting.

There is a wide range of agencies out there, from the international 'superagencies' which handle everyone from the hottest Hollywood star to the latest soap heart-throb, to the one-person-band type of agency which keeps pubs and clubs in a steady stream of tribute acts. Some of these agencies focus on acting and singing and some also look after dancers. There are also specialist dance agencies, sometimes attached to the larger dance studios. Dance teachers and choreographers may act as agents in their own right, using their students and contacts as a client base. And there are also 'entertainment agencies' which, strictly speaking, don't look after any specific performers but in effect act as sub-contractors to people who are organising any kind of event from a wedding to a product launch. You identify the act or individual you want to perform at your event; these agents will locate them and book them. Dancers are often required, so it is well worth your while letting such agencies know that you are on the market.

It is not unknown for boyfriends, girlfriends, mums and dads of dancers to act as their agent – or to offer to. We are not saying that such arrangements can never work, but as with most relationships where friends and family members get involved in business together, it is even more important to get everything agreed on paper. When a straightforward business arrangement comes to a close, either amicably or otherwise, the parties involved eventually lick their wounds and go their separate ways. But when there is a family or friendship relationship at stake the fallout can be much nastier and last for years.

Here are some basic questions you need to ask anyone or any agency offering to represent you, whether you have known them all your life or are meeting them for the first time. (How ready they are to give you honest and full answers to these questions is a good indication of how suitable they will be for doing business with.)

How established is the agent or agency?
The longer you are in the dance business and the more successful jobs you do, the more you will build up your reputation. The same applies to agents and agencies. While production companies are always on the lookout for new talent, they don't necessarily have the time or resources to search for it themselves; contacting an

established agency means they can be reasonably sure that every dancer on its books will be of the required standard. Producers and agents often build up relationships so that when there is a particular need for a certain type of dancer, the producer goes to their favourite agent(s) as a first stop. From your point of view, signing on with an established and well-respected agency means some of that reputation obviously rubs off on you.

Does it follow that you should never sign up with a newer agency, or with one which has just started up? Not necessarily, but you should take a close look at the people behind it. In some cases they may be successful dancers themselves; in others they may have been working for the more established agencies and branched out into their own niche. These individuals may well work harder with the first dancers they take on, and this could certainly have a knock-on benefit in getting you work. But be wary of agents who are vague about their experience in the business (that's the *dance* business – their experience in other areas of showbusiness isn't necessarily relevant), or who make big promises without any concrete evidence to back them up.

What kind of clients do they already have?

Obviously, an agency whose clients include established dancers and dance groups must be doing something right. However, bear in mind that the nature of the dance industry is such that dancers, especially the busier ones, may be on the books of several different agents. Consider asking which agent is getting the bulk of the work for that particular artist ...

What kind of work does the agency get for its clients?

Finding this out is important, not just in terms of weeding out the 'talkers' from the 'doers' but also because there are particular types of job that play more to your individual strengths, and fit in better with your own career vision. It makes sense therefore to sign with agencies which specialise in getting that type of work for their clients. Like different dancers, different agencies have their own areas of strength. If you enjoy cruise work and are on the books of a particular agency which specialises in this area, you may also want to do some television – but perhaps this isn't one of their strong points. You may therefore also seek out a connection with an agent who has contacts in TV. The agencies themselves usually like to focus on their strong markets, so they won't object to you doing work through other agents in different areas – unless of course you double-book yourself!

If you are 'upfront' with your agent and they are 'upfront' with you, there should be no problems on either side. On the other hand if you have a 'control freak' agent who gets paranoid about you working with other people, this is a big danger sign. At best we would suggest that this agent needs to be bringing you in so much work that you don't have time for any other contracts, before they have the right to start complaining. The worst-case scenario (and sadly not an uncommon one) is that you hook up with someone who is managing other people's lives as a substitute for sorting out their own. In such a situation you are better off terminating the relationship immediately.

How will the agency promote you?

This is a particularly important question these days, since there are many scam agencies on the lookout for the desperate and the unwary. Yes, it is your responsibility to pay for your basic promotional materials such as photographs, and to keep the agency supplied with copies; but in general, since the agency makes its money out of the work that you do, it should cover the costs of promoting you and possess the contacts you need but don't have. Be very wary if their promotional methods involve 'special and expensive photoshoots' or putting you on a website with hundreds of other performers (in other words, things you could probably do yourself with more focus and at less cost).

How much commission does the agent charge?

Agent commissions vary depending on the kind of work involved, but are usually somewhere in the region of 10–30 per cent. If someone offers you an 80–20 split (as in *their* 80 and *your* 20) as they did to a friend of ours recently, you are definitely in the hands of either a scam artist or a fantasist.

Never pay any upfront fee to join an agency; this is the second sign of a scam artist. (The first sign is over-the-top, gushing flattery of your talents and big unrealistic claims for what the agency can do for you ... all designed to get you to pay a joining fee.) Legitimate agencies believe in their clients and in their own ability to find those clients work, so they don't need to charge a joining fee. For the same reason they usually have more than enough clients on their books and have no need to beg you to come on board.

More to the point, the agency you approach may be concerned to ensure that each client gets proper attention and therefore reluctant to expand its list beyond the number it can cope with. Ironically, this may be just the kind of agency that will best serve your interests. If they like you, and it really is a case that there simply isn't enough room on their books at present, make it *your* business to remind them that you are still interested after a few months. You don't need to be pushy: an email or card whenever you're doing something interesting will suffice, particularly if there is an opportunity for them to come along and see you performing. (You should be doing this for all the important people on your mailing list anyhow.) Circumstances and client rosters do change, and your reminder could arrive at just the right time.

In fact the 'reminding' process is just as important a part of your initial marketing – be it to agents or to independent contacts – as the preparation of the individual promotional items themselves. You research your markets, you prepare your pitch, you send off your promotional package ... and if you don't hear anything after a week or so, you call up to see if it has arrived. Perhaps it has, but the answer is 'No'. So you do some new research, polish up your package if necessary, and send it out again. Make sure that all the time you are going through this cycle you are attending your classes and workouts and continuing to hone your dance abilities. This is not just to keep you motivated: one of these days you are going to get a letter or a phone call which is *not* a knockback. When that audition or interview does come up, you'll be ready – and the next chapter will help you make the most of it.

Chapter Four

Stepping Out

Auditions and talent shows

We would love to guarantee that the information in this chapter
will ensure you success in every interview, audition or talent
show you go up for. There are several e-books and systems
advertised on the Internet and elsewhere which promise just
that: however, it's not a promise that we could make in good
conscience (and in our opinion you should be careful of anyone
else making such claims, too). The truth is that there will always
be more good dancers than there are good jobs – and the better
and more prestigious the job, the more numerous and more
qualified the dancers who will turn up for it.

What one director or choreographer likes may not please
another, so there is really no one 'system' that is foolproof. At
the beginning of your career, the more auditions you attend, the
better – just to get the experience of auditioning and the various
ways in which these events are organised. One thing you will
quickly learn is that while the individual details and set-up of
each audition or other trial may vary, there are basic pointers
and common business courtesies that you can observe which
will mark you out as an employable professional. While you
may not automatically be numbered among the stars, you can
certainly distance yourself from the 'crowd' – the people who
have a showbusiness dream but who are not prepared to work
hard enough to make that dream come true.

Types of audition

As the name suggests, the open audition is an opportunity for
anyone to try their luck at becoming part of the show. It would
be untrue to say that professional dancers don't get decent parts
from open auditions; talent will always shine out. However, you

need to be aware that there may well be hundreds of other people at such an audition, many of whom are far more interested in the (so-called) glamour of showbiz or the big break than working to build a career. This is particularly true now that *Pop Idol* types of audition shows have become the norm on television. It is also a fact that such open auditions tend to generate a lot of publicity for live shows and forthcoming TV productions, especially in the regions, so it is not unknown for companies who have already hired their quota of principal dancers and performers to hold auditions as much to generate this publicity boost as to find extra cast members.

The nature of an open audition is such that it can be very much a 'cattle call' process. Depending on the numbers that have turned up, you may get a very short time in which to show what you can do, and the casting directors or choreographers are liable to make snap decisions. Bear in mind that while anyone can turn up to an open audition, the ads often list some general requirements such as a height or age range. This may be because of the nature of the show, or because the costumes you will be wearing will be mass-produced rather than tailored for you. If you differ radically from such specifications, spare yourself some heartache and promote your talents elsewhere.

A private or closed audition will usually be a smaller affair, and those attending will usually have been sent along by an agent. From the company's point of view, using agents means that the prospective dancers have already been pre-selected as meeting the various requirements for the job. From your point of view, you will at least know that the casting director and choreographer have expressed an interest in seeing you personally – and you will probably have a little more time to show what you can do than you would if there were hundreds of hopefuls. If the production is a reasonably sized one, the fact that they have taken the trouble to hold private auditions could also mean that the parts on offer are good ones. While it is more likely that you will end up at a private audition through the recommendation of an agent, you may also find yourself being invited to one as a result of having written to the production company with your details at just the right time (see also Chapter Three on self-marketing).

Preparing for an audition

As an actor, you would normally go to audition knowing that the people you need to impress are the director, the producer, the casting director or some combination of all three. As a dancer you may find that there is a much wider range of individuals who have a say in whether you are successful or not. For a musical or theatre show, for example, while the choice of dancers may be left to the choreographer, there may also be 'hands on' directors and producers who want their opinions taken on board. If you are auditioning for a commercial shoot, the client and the advertising agency may be after a certain 'look' which in some cases may be even more important to them than your dance prowess. Treat them the same as you would any other audience: as a dancer you can't predict, control or worry about who you have to perform in front of, you just need to focus on giving the best possible account of yourself each time. And putting that presentation together is as much about what you do *before* an audition – or a performance – as what you do when you get there.

We have heard various theories about how to approach auditions, from dancers and from other performers; the following advice is based on what works for us and for the people we know. But there is one attitude prevalent among performers that *definitely* doesn't work for us, whether we are performing ourselves or auditioning other performers – and that is the idea that it is somehow 'cool' not to make the maximum effort to get the job once you have made the commitment to turn up to the audition. Perhaps the maxim that 'a great performer holds something back at rehearsal so they can give their all on opening night' has somehow got confused with auditions in people's heads, but take it from us, if you are not prepared to put as much effort into your audition preparations as you would into opening night, you may never make it to rehearsal. (Of course, now that we are off our hobby horse, you might also note the flipside of that warning: if you do put a little extra effort into your preparation, you will be giving yourself a big advantage over quite a few auditionees before you even turn up.)

The right image

We will look in detail later on in the book at your health and general wellbeing, as they are such important elements in sustaining a successful dance career. But when you are searching for the auditions to get that career kick-started, you need to view your general health and appearance as an important marketing tool. Just as you need to keep yourself fit to be able to do whatever dance work comes your way effectively, so you need to ensure that in terms of both image and appearance, you are ready for any audition opportunities that may arise. Like a top photographer who is no good without their camera, you may not have the time to 'scrub up' in time to take advantage of an unexpected opportunity – you need to have your show 'ready to roll' at all times.

At a very basic level, you need to be conscious of keeping your appearance up to scratch even when you are not working. You are in showbusiness – which means you need to act like you are permanently on show. It *doesn't* mean that you have to become obsessed with your looks, but you do need to keep your hair, nails and other elements of your image in top condition at all times. And no, that doesn't involve spending large amounts of money that you haven't got: eating healthily and basic grooming should be more than enough to keep you in shape.

Your dance clothes need to be in shape, too – they are an important part of your image. While 'weathered' gear and equipment may be the mark of a seasoned professional in sports and even in music, the same definitely doesn't apply in the dance world. You have a very short timeframe in which to stand out at each audition, and a striking outfit can give you a little extra help just when it is needed. By striking we don't necessarily mean garish or over-the-top: choose something that stands out but is also compatible with your own style and skin colour. Take the same approach with make-up. On the one hand you want to avoid looking pale and washed-out – studio and theatrical lighting is rarely very kind to the beginner – but you don't want the 'plastered on' look either. As you become practised at doing auditions, you'll be able to note how certain dancers have looks and styles that make them stand out from the crowd without appearing to try too hard, and you will certainly get ideas. However, avoid copying someone's style directly, even if it is working for them. It may not work for you – and in any case you want to be distinctive as well as noticeable.

Another factor to bear in mind is the kind of audition you are going for. You may not always have much information before turning up, but if you do know that there is a certain theme to the job or show, it can make a difference if you wear something which is in the same vein – always remembering that you will probably have to dance at some point. Tight trousers may show off your great legs and terrific behind, but unless you can actually move in them, you'll be better off targeting modelling assignments than jobs which involve actual dancing. Obviously this goes double for the shoes you wear.

In addition to your clothes and shoes, the other essential item you will need to bring with you is your bag. While actors may be able to travel light ('Just me and my talent, darling!'), those of us in the musical side of the profession usually find ourselves not only having to look glamorous, but having to do so while carrying something heavy. If your bag is not quite the size of a double bass, it can certainly feel like that sometimes with the accumulation of the gear that dancers end up carrying. Besides make-up, changes of clothes and shoes, you may well find that after hanging around for long periods just waiting for your turn to audition, you make snacks, drinks and books (this one in particular, we hope!) essential parts of your kit. If you have a marketing pack (see also Chapter Three) it certainly makes sense to carry a few extra copies with you at all times – you never know when the opportunity for a little pre- or post-audition net-working may arise. Also, you don't want to discover that you've left the one copy of the pack you've brought specifically for the audition on the bus. (This probably applies to open auditions more than to closed ones; for the latter you are likely to have been called in because your pack has already done its work.)

It goes without saying that with all that stuff crammed in it, your bag needs to be one that won't burst as you stumble into the dance studio (not the kind of striking entrance we are recommending). As it's also likely to see a lot of wear and tear, it's worth investing in a bag that can 'go the distance'. Looking the part applies to your accessories, too. Finally, make sure your bag can be carried comfortably, no matter how full it is. If it is properly adjusted with comfortable handles or straps, you are less likely to throw your posture out and/or damage your back. Oh, and label your bag: it may be distinctive, but when there are a couple of hundred of them strewn around an audition venue, the inevitable sometimes happens.

Be on time

It should come as no surprise that no matter what kind of audition you are attending, the number one rule is to be on time. In the world of showbusiness, time is money; when you are working, any lateness on your part will inevitably cause problems and expense not just for your fellow performers, but for entire stage and TV productions too. So it's best to establish right from the audition stage that you are a good timekeeper. Admittedly, people do turn up late for open auditions, and if they are suitably apologetic or charming or plain hard-nosed they can still get seen. However, the danger of getting into this habit is that it may also become your norm at private auditions, and that is certainly a reputation you don't want to acquire.

Even if you are normally on time for things, it is well worth putting in a little more preparation before an important interview to make sure that nothing goes wrong (and let's face it, at the beginning of your dance career *every* interview is an important interview). We are about to talk about some very simple steps, which you may well dismiss as *too* simple. Don't. We know too many people (including us) who have come to grief by taking them for granted.

1 Double-check the time and the venue for the audition. If possible check out one of the Internet sites such as www.streetmap.co.uk or www.maporama.com which will give you a detailed route to the venue from wherever you are starting out. Calculate the time it will take you to get to the venue – and then allow enough extra time to handle any unforeseen circumstances such as breakdowns or public-transport delays.

2 If at all possible get a contact phone number for the venue, so that if you are running late you can call ahead and let someone know. And yes, we know that with lots of dancers lining up to do their bit your phone call may not be regarded as necessary or even important – but you are far less likely to

be penalised for making an unnecessary call to say you will be late than for turning up sweaty and flustered, only to find that you have missed your slot. Instead of moving you back, the organisers may have either 'bounced' you or simply packed up and gone. (If you tend to overuse your mobile and be in frequent 'no credit/can't call out' binds, try to ration your phone use when you know you have an audition coming up – or at least save enough money for a pre-pay card.)

3 Don't assume, simply because you have reached the venue, that you are on time. While auditions do take place in theatres, studios and other designated performance spaces, we have also known them to be in venues as mundane as community centres and as unexpected as military barracks. If the venue is big, you may need to allow extra time for finding the actual room you are supposed to strut your stuff in. Your chances of securing a place in the latest West End show will not be helped if you accidentally end up in the middle of an expectant mums' aerobics class or a hand-to-hand combat course.

Dealing with your nerves

At last! You've made it to the venue and the audition proper is about to start. This is your moment. How do you feel? Excited? Energised? Terrified? Welcome to the club. When we work with actors, even famous and seasoned ones, coping with audition nerves is certainly a factor: after all there may be 20 or 30 other performers up for the same plum part. How much more daunting, then, to be a beginner or even an experienced dancer confronted with an audition where there may well be hundreds of dancers up for the job, each with just a few short minutes to clinch it. Those old insecurities tend to kick in, sometimes with a vengeance, as soon as you enter the audition room. There are liable to be a lot of good-looking, agile people lined up. Some of them may even be dancers you recognise, and it is not unusual to see people pulling some sharp moves as their 'warm up' that you would be hard-pressed to reproduce in full performance flow.

The truth of the matter is that no matter how experienced you are, there is a pretty good chance that several people in the room have more dancing experience and maybe even more talent than you. But take heart from the fact that the most highly qualified and experienced dancers are often far less confident than you might think. To them, even the rawest beginner can look like just as much of a threat. They don't *act* on this fear, though – they have learned to recognise it as natural performer's anxiety. Instead of allowing it to distract from their focus, they use it to spur themselves on to give their very best performance. You can do the same thing.

Because large auditions are such a feature of the dancer's life, not all prospective dancers are tough enough to persevere through the first year of auditioning. Having turned up to one too many auditions with no success, they decide that there are easier ways to make a living and hang up their dancing shoes, letting go of their dancing dreams. Of course, there is always a whole new wave of hopefuls to take their place – but precisely because there is such a turnover in dancers, the ones who do stay the course tend to get to know each other quickly. They will certainly become familiar faces to each other at all the big auditions: they may well have danced in the chorus together in several tours and shows, and it's possible that they may even have worked with this particular choreographer or director before and be a 'known quantity'. If you are a 'newbie' on the audition circuit it can be a bit daunting to feel that everyone else knows each other, and knows 'the form'. Don't let it get to you – as your career progresses you'll develop your own circle of friends and your own network. You'll also find that, contrary to the stereotype, there are fewer prima donnas in dance than you might think. If you are genuine and straightforward you will probably find quite a few more seasoned auditioners willing to guide you on what to do and when. If you can't pluck up the courage to ask, at least keep your eyes glued to some of the more confident-looking people and do what they do.

Above all, bear in mind that just because someone knows the choreographer or the director, it doesn't necessarily mean that they are guaranteed to be chosen. It might just be that the production needs something fresh and individual and new, and that you are just the person to give it to them. You certainly need to believe in yourself – be confident that you have talent to offer which will shine, no matter what your level of experience. And if you can't quite convince yourself of this yet, at least *pretend* you believe it and the actual belief may kick in later.

Showbusiness is all about make-believe, remember? While you are focusing on yourself, though – hopefully on your strengths, and not your nerves – remember to keep the major part of your attention on the choreographer or whoever is in charge of the audition. A dance studio can be a very visual place, but Jenny maintains that one of the key dance skills is the ability to *listen*.

What happens at audition?

At some point the audition proper will be called to order. Auditions can follow different formats based on the type of show and the number of people attending, but most go something like this:

- The choreographer will explain as much as you need to know about the nature of the job you are trying out for. (Details can sometimes be sketchy, perhaps because it is a high-profile show and the producers want to keep the content secret until opening night. It's not unheard of for the script of a musical to still be in progress while auditions are going on.)
- There will then be a demonstration of the steps you are being asked to learn for the audition, usually on their own and then in time to the music. This is one of the reasons why we encourage you to get to auditions early if you can. In a crowded studio or confined space filled with a lot of dancers, it can be difficult to get a good look at the moves you are being asked to make. If you do find yourself stuck at the back, pray that the choreographer is the kind that will move the crowd around so that those further behind get a good look too – but be prepared to 'wing it' as best you can if not (again, it helps to have already identified some more experienced dancers so that you can watch what they do … but double-check with a few rather than with just one, in case you've picked someone who's not as good at observing as their confidence would suggest).
- The next stage usually involves the assembled dancers being given some time to practise the steps for themselves. Although some people will be chatty and looking for a fun experience, the more focused beginner is going to take this time seriously and really try to get those steps locked in. Even simple steps

and routines can be hard to remember when they are demonstrated quickly and when you have to learn them under pressure. Welcome to the world of professional dance.

Just to make you even more uncomfortable, we may as well let you know that while this is your private practice time, the client/judges may already be casting their eyes over the crowd: remember that these days, they are increasingly searching for the right 'look' as much as for the top dancing talent. On the other hand, be encouraged that that 'look' often has more to do with confidence, professionalism and attitude then just physical appearance. Regardless of what the panel are talking about or where they are pointing, you can't know what's going on inside their heads, so it's far more useful to focus on what's going on inside *yours* – and more specifically getting those steps in there. In the short space of time you will be given, it may not be possible to make them second nature. But the more smoothly you can do them, the more likely you will be able to give a 'dancing' performance rather than just a 'remembering' one.

- The assembled dancers will then be given numbers and broken up into smaller groups so that the judges can get a good look (however brief) at each dancer. If there is a very big group at the audition, it may be that half those attending are sent away for a second session later. (During this chapter you'll notice that we use lots of different words, from 'judge' to 'interviewer' to 'choreographer', to describe the members of the panel which decides whether or not you get through. That's because the make-up of each individual panel *is* different. It's your job to give your all, no matter who is in the driver's seat.)

- *Showtime!* The waiting is finally over – your group takes to the floor and you get to give your all in front of the selection panel and all of the other dancers (we're not sure which element is more nerve-wracking for a beginner – the dancing or the watching). If you are dancing in a small group, do try to use all of your floor-craft and spatial awareness to make sure that the judges get a good look at you, particularly if you find yourself at the back. However, do so gracefully – you don't want to look like you are pushy or not a team player, as being able to fit into the troupe is just as important a skill as the actual dancing.

- Sometimes the panel will make a selection right away; sometimes your group will be asked to dance several times. After that the decision, when it comes, is liable to be swift and not necessarily painless. The dancers who fit the bill will be asked to stay; for the others it will be a brief 'thank you very much for coming' and time for the long walk to get changed. If you do make it to the second round of the selection process, congratulations. Now you'll have to go through the whole experience again as the group gets whittled down to the chosen few!

While less crowded, the closed or invitation-only audition will tend to follow more or less the same format as the open audition – although since the selectors have already expressed an interest in seeing you, there may be slightly more scope to show yourself to good advantage. On the other hand, if they are looking for a certain 'type', you may find yourself in a room full of dancers who look not dissimilar to you! (John once attended an audition and had to share the waiting room with 20 or so other balding men with Irish accents.) Your challenge then is to really communicate the spark that makes you stand out from the crowd – and in order to communicate it, you will have had to work it out and practise it long beforehand.

You may be given some indication of how you have done at the end of this kind of audition, just as you would for the open kind. Equally, though, the panel may want to do some deliberating, so you may be sent away none the wiser and only hear the result via your agent. While you may not be pleased to be dismissed with a curt 'thank you' at an open audition, at least then you know you haven't got the part. If you are waiting to hear back after an audition and *don't* hear back after a reasonable period of time, you can usually assume that you haven't been chosen on this occasion.

Coping with rejection

As we said at the beginning of this chapter, there is no magic formula for getting through a dance audition. Really working hard on your ability to learn steps quickly can give you an edge. In an audition where image is a primary factor, making sure that you are looking your best can make the difference. Since you never know exactly what a selector is looking for (and in many auditions, a number of them may be looking for quite different things), aiming for the highest standards in *every* area of your operation will give you the best chance. Each audition you attend gives you another chance to reach and surpass those standards, to show that unlike the aspiring dancers who drop out when success isn't instant, you have the vision and drive to go the distance.

If you do have that vision and drive, you may well find it even more painful when you get knocked out in the early audition rounds. Although your eyes may be smarting, we urge you not to pack up and leave – no matter how much you may want to. Stay around and continue to watch the other audition rounds for as long as you can. Watch each set of dancers closely and pretend that you are on the selection panel. Who would you take to the next round, and who would you send away with a 'thanks but no thanks'? Why? See if the judges' decision tallies with yours. If it doesn't the first time, it should be easier to work out what they are looking for with each new selection. Once you've identified the 'x factor' that seems to work for each chosen dancer, ask yourself if there is a lesson there that you could apply to your own work. This is *not* the same as copying someone else's style outright: in fact, the most 'individual' performers are often those who have combined influences from a number of different sources in a new and exciting way.

Obviously, not everyone has the commitment or courage to learn from rejection, so if you find you are one of the few people left observing as the audition draws to a close, do remember to smile a lot. You want people to realise that you are a dancer interested in improving your art, not a vengeful auditionee waiting to take revenge on the selection panel!

While encouraging you to use each audition as a learning experience, we are fully aware that your aim is, and should be, to actually get the parts you go for. We certainly don't expect you to enjoy the experience of getting rejected, and if we're honest, no matter how long you stay in the business and no matter how many successes you have, the occasional rejection (which still happens to the stars every so often, too) is no more fun after 20 years in the business than it is for the dancer starting out. It's how you handle the knock-backs that make you a real performer – not avoiding them in the first place. All great performers put themselves on the line in their work ... so when that work gets rejected, it is only natural to feel personally rejected too. To make matters worse, most of the time you won't get any feedback as to why you didn't make it. So unless you did something really obvious like forget the steps or tread on a fellow dancer during your audition piece (and even that may not have been the factor that got you bounced), you may never know why you didn't get that particular audition.

There are two common reactions to failure, neither of which is useful to your career progress. The first is to assume that you were passed over because you just weren't good enough. Certainly, the job may have gone to a more experienced dancer: as we have been saying all through this chapter, constant auditioning and practising is your route to gaining the same level of experience for yourself. But it may have been some entirely different factor that influenced the judges' decision. This is particularly true of open auditions – after all, if the requirement is specifically for blonde dancers, even the best brunette may not get very far. And for a 'teeny' type show, the preference may be for particularly waif-like dancers, no matter what their actual age is. (As we have already noted, it is worth checking the original ad for any specific requirements so that you avoid going for totally unsuitable auditions. Equal opportunities and other such legis- lation may prevent some requirements from being listed in adverts, but inevitably they will be in the selectors' minds when they are doing the choosing.) So not getting chosen may not be as much your fault as you think. Of course, we are not suggesting that you shouldn't check your performance against your own highest standards: you'll usually know when you have done a bad gig. However, even if this is the case, you are far better off getting back into practice and working to make sure the next one goes better than beating yourself up for the rest of the year.

The other reaction to rejection is almost the complete opposite of feeling down, and though it may have short-term benefits it is ultimately just as damaging. This is the 'How dare they, they don't recognise great talent when they see it' reaction – usually accompanied by the immortal words, 'I'll show them!'. It's certainly true that picking yourself up, dusting yourself off and starting all over again is the time-honoured way of coping with showbusiness knock-backs – but be very careful that when you do start all over again, you start back on the path towards your original career vision, not on some crusade to show all the people who said you could never do it that they were wrong. In the first place, they *didn't* say you could never be a dancer; they just decided that you weren't right for a particular part. And even if they did say something negative (and there are certainly Simon Cowells in the dance world too), the most successful performers have developed the ability to listen objectively to *every* comment on their work. You don't have to agree with what everyone tells you – in fact, even when the advice is genuinely well-meaning you will often find yourself fielding two different suggestions from two equally qualified sources. It is your job to weigh up all the options and directions open to you and to choose the path that works best for your particular career: after all, nobody can direct your career except you. But you can't make the best career choices if anger or over-sensitivity stops you listening to all the choices available to you.

Auditioning for other jobs

Before we leave the subject of auditions, we did mention in Chapter Two on dancers' jobs that there are quite a few activities dancers can get involved in to make a living which, while they use dance skills, aren't strictly dance-related. Getting these jobs may also involve interviews and casting sessions – and, nerve-wracking as it may be to have to dance in front of critical audiences, some dancers find having to do 'talking' auditions even more scary.

Perhaps the most terrifying experience of all for the dancer is the kind of interview where instead of being asked to demonstrate their performance skills, the interviewer simply wants to have a chat and ask questions. No matter how informal and relaxed the interview may appear, you haven't simply been called in for a chat; how you answer the questions will have a direct bearing on whether or not you get the job. But just like in a performance audition, since you don't know exactly what the clients are looking for, it's best to relax, smile and answer the questions as fully and confidently as you can.

Do look for clues in the questions, though. If the interviewer asks you if you have any experience of sports or martial arts when you are auditioning for, say, a musical based on a Shakespeare play, it may be that this is an updated version and those skills may be incorporated into the dance routines. If you do have experience of those activities, it's well worth mentioning it. On the other hand, while you might not be the world's sportiest dancer, you may have done well in a street-dance competition. Tangential as this may seem, it will do you no harm to bring it up, especially if you can make the connection for the interviewer to show that this would give you an edge when learning that kind of routine.

Answer the questions as honestly as you can. If you have no or little experience of a particular style or skill, say so – and focus on what a fast learner you are. If the job really doesn't suit you and is way beyond your current experience and capabilities, it is far better to let it go than to get a reputation for being a big talker but a poor deliverer.

Auditions to camera

At a TV or film casting the audition process is essentially the same, the only difference being that instead of performing for and talking to a choreographer or a casting director, you will be performing directly to camera. The more you work with cameras, the more you will get used to them. The main challenge for most people is that the less experienced they are, the more they feel the need to 'act like a performer' rather than simply relaxing and being 'themselves with the volume turned up' which is the technique used by most seasoned performers.

In the absence of experience, a 'quick trick' to help you appear slightly more natural is to simply imagine that the camera is not a camera at all, but someone you really like, feel comfortable with and would really like to impress with your dancing or performing. Some performers have been known to actually tape a photo of such a person on to the camera. Obviously you won't be able to do that at an audition, but if you can mentally replace the camera with the same image, the trick should still work.

Recalls/call-backs

If you do make it past the first audition, casting or screen test, don't book your holiday in the sun just yet. There may well be a number of call-backs while the producers whittle down the shortlist. In very big shows, particularly Broadway to West End transfers with large amounts of money riding on their success or failure, the producers can be very picky about finding a cast who can do the show exactly as it was done at home. In one such show virtually every prominent black actress/dancer in Britain was auditioned for one of the principal roles; many were called back again and again (turning down other work in the process); and the company still went with an American performer for the opening six months.

Depending on your personality, being recalled may be more or less pressure than your original audition. On the one hand, now you know you have something that appeals to the producers, so your quest to become a working dancer has advanced one big step. On the other hand, you also know that the average quality of dancer competing in this next round will be much higher. They may already have decided to give you the job, and this new audition is a chance to see how all of the potential cast members interact together on the dance floor – or they may have been impressed with your performance but fearful that it was a fluke, so they are calling you back to watch for any mistakes you might make.

In general we recommend that you approach a call-back with exactly the same level of preparation and attention to detail as you did the original audition. Don't be complacent: the job may not be as 'in the bag' as you think. Equally, don't be too apprehensive – you have the same talents today as you had on the day you won the call-back. From the point of view of style, it's usually best to make sure you look the same at the call-back as you did on the day of your original audition. This helps the judges to remember what they liked about you in the first place.

A recall audition/interview is usually a little longer and more detailed than a first audition: the client will want to know you better. Again, be prepared for any clues as to what they are looking for in the questions that they ask and directions that they give. Be ready to rummage in your mental and physical box of tricks to find the element that makes you the right person for the job.

Finally the glorious day will arrive when the auditions and call-backs have done their job and you (or your agent) will get the good news that the job is yours. Whether it's a one-off job or a long-term contract, you now have an opportunity to gain some solid performance experience, a shiny new entry for your CV, and of course some much-needed cash ... all of which will come in handy at the end of this contract when you are back on the audition circuit again.

Talent shows

Thanks to the popularity of shows like *Pop Idol*, the process of auditioning – which used to happen behind closed doors – has become a popular spectator sport (in the same way that throwing people to the lions used to be a popular spectator sport, some might say). In addition to auditions, dance competitions and talent shows have always been a possible route into the world of showbusiness. Today such competitions are increasingly high-profile; there are even televised dance talent shows such as *Bump and Grind*, and the line between amateur entrants and professionals seeking other ways to find work is becoming more blurred.

Just as with auditions, turning up for talent contests and competitions also means that you are likely to be turned *down*. Every judge is looking for different things, some of which you may be able to provide and some of which you won't. Different styles of dance and different types of dancer go in and out of fashion, and public competitions tend to focus much more on what is popular than on what is best technically. So if you find getting turned down at auditions upsetting, putting yourself through the same thing in front of the public may not appeal to you. However, if your aim is to be a working dancer you're going to have to learn to please the public at some time or another, and contests are a great way to get practice in front of real audiences early in your career – particularly if you learn to enjoy the experience and don't get too hung up about winning.

There are one or two things you *can* do to increase your chances of winning. One obvious way is to find out in advance about the kind of competition you are up against. If the talent contest you've entered for is holding several heats, it makes a lot of sense to try to get along to one of these in advance of your own slot. It will give you a very good idea of the format of the show, the standard of the acts and the kind of audience you can expect.

If the talent show is for dancers only, try and get a feel for the range of styles represented. For example, if street dance is the norm, you'll need to make sure there's something about *your* street dance that is superior, or at least memorably different, from that of the competition. If your style of dance is very different, it can either work to your advantage (novelty value) or be *so* different that the audience and judges don't know how to take it. This is where a little imagination and showbusiness flare comes in: a talent show is a *show*, not an audition. A ballet or jazz dancer might easily win a street-dance type of competition by performing in classical style but adopting a street image, or perhaps by combining a few very 'street' moves into their more formal style.

If the contest is a more general one, featuring singers or comedians too, being a dancer will be an advantage because you are likely to be in a minority. But remember that the singers and comics will be talking to the audience as part of their acts, and building a relationship with the audience in this kind of contest can make all the difference. If you haven't already learned to connect with your audience just as powerfully through your dance performance, talent contests are a great way to hone that skill … and an even better demonstration of why this skill is necessary!

If you do get to an early heat of the contest, try to put yourself in the mind of a judge watching the other dancers. What do they do that impresses you; do you like their attitude, dress or dance style? Is there anything you can learn and apply to your own act? Equally, what do other acts do that annoys you? Put a little practice time in after you've finished your research and see if you can incorporate the good stuff you learned into your own act – and more important, avoid making some of the obvious mistakes. Did you feel that the performer was ignoring you at any point in their act? Now think about your own act: is there any point at which people on one or other side of the hall might feel that you are ignoring *them*? If so, and given that you can't be in two places at once, what do you do about it? Solving the problem in a way that suits your own style not only gives you a tool that you can use in contests, it will also be really helpful in auditions and shows later on.

A common question about talent contests is, 'Where, in the running order, is it best to go on?'. You may not be given the choice, or it may be that the act that turns up first gets to pick their place in the running order. In a variety-style show, the organisers may well adjust the running order to slot in specialty acts between every two singers (or whichever type of act is over-represented), which is a good thing for all concerned. Dance is often seen as a good way to open or close a show, so you may be slotted in at the beginning or at the end of the night. But if you *do* get the chance to choose where you go on the bill, pick the position that *you* are most comfortable with. If you work hard at your act and build up your confidence in your talent, you'll shine *whenever* you go onstage. Which means it's up to you to weigh up the pros and cons of the positions that suit you best.

For instance, it's true that nobody particularly enjoys going on first, when the audience isn't properly warmed-up. But by going on first, you also avoid having to sit through the rest of the night racked with pre-show nerves. If the talent show is being decided by an audience or a judges' vote at the end, going on first may mean that at the end of the evening even the most dazzling opening performance may have faded into distant memory. In a professional show, going on last is the sign of the 'bill topper', the star of the show – and certainly, if you can pull a dazzling performance out of the bag in this slot it will be very fresh in the voters' minds when it comes to decision time. But the inevitable delays and false starts that dog all but the most highly organised talent shows can also mean that it can be very hard to keep focused and energetic until the final curtain. This applies not just to the performers, but to the audience and judges too.

Unlike singers or comics, you as a dancer don't have to fear someone singing the same song or telling the same joke you were going to. Even if someone else uses the same track for their spot before you go on, your routines are going to be radically different. Or at least they will be if you haven't both copied them move for move from the latest Beyonce video. *Don't* copy your moves from even the most popular video: if it is popular enough, most of the audience will have been busy practising it too. Always bring your own style to whatever you do.

When judging time comes around, try not to focus so much on whether you've won or lost, but concentrate instead on what you've *learned* from this particular competition. Don't assume that because you didn't win a particular heat, you haven't impressed anyone: if there are any talent scouts at the show, and particularly any good ones, they are there to spot potential – not necessarily just someone who is good at winning a particular type of competition. They might spot *you*. So have your business cards and your marketing material packed ready in your dancer's bag to hand out in case anyone expresses interest in seeing you again. And then get busy practising for the next audition or talent show.

When all that practice finally pays off and *you're* the winner (and who's to say that won't happen sooner rather than later?), you may be asked to do an encore. Don't worry about trying to 'top' your previous performance or show off, just dance the dance that won you your victory in the first place.

One final caution: do read the entry conditions carefully of any talent shows you enter, especially those which include *agency or management contracts* as prizes. It's perfectly possible that a credible agency or management company may choose the talent-show route to recruit new acts. But *your* aim in signing any contract is to get the best deal for you as a performer, because you can be sure that the company or person offering the contract will have set it up to protect *their* interests already. Make sure that you're not signing away your right to run your own career by signing up to enter a contest. The thing you'll want to focus on when running your own career is its long-term future, not just the gigs and opportunities you are focusing on now. The secret of turning success at auditions and talent shows into a long-term successful career that's worth managing is to consistently turn in great performances. In the next chapter we'll be getting advice from some dancers who have reached that level, and have the successful careers to match.

Chapter Five

Dance into the Fire

What makes a great dance performance?

As we have been suggesting throughout this book – and as we suggest to every performer, be they a dancer, a singer or a double-jointed elephant juggler – the same principles which apply to success in any kind of business also apply to showbusiness. Anyone who is serious about making a living out of performing can see the truth of this: after all, it makes sense that no matter how talented a dancer you are, if you don't market those talents sufficiently, or manage your financial affairs effectively, you will be in no position either to create opportunities, or to take advantage of them when they arise.

But what about the 'performance' part of performing? Surely that's where the 'magic' of showbusiness kicks in; isn't success or failure in performance entirely down to a dancer's talent, the attitude of the audience, dumb luck and various other factors which are not within our direct control? Not quite. A set of rules and regulations followed to the letter certainly doesn't guarantee a successful dance performance, but equally there is a lot that can be done, both beforehand and 'in the moment', to help enable one. As with any other business, while marketing, good management and perseverance can generate work, what gets you work time and time again and again is consistently delivering a first-class product.

To get you thinking about how to achieve that success factor in your performances, we asked some established working dancers to describe the attitudes and approaches that have helped build their thriving careers. (The questions are from John, and are designed to help you apply people's answers to your own development.)

Question 1: What, for you, is the key to a great dance performance?

David Watson is a dancer and choreographer based in the UK:

In my opinion, the key to a great performance is being fully connected with what you are performing – as well as understanding what you are performing as fully as possible.

Jacquie Bird is a singer, dancer, actress, choreographer and dance instructor. Her extensive career includes Broadway musicals and films such as *School Daze* (director, Spike Lee) and *Cotton Club*:

The key for me is dancing from the soul. Today there is so much emphasis on tricks and technical capabilities, but after you extend your leg up to your ear a few times I get bored and want to know: What else do you have to show me? What do you have to say? What are you dancing about? *Why* are you dancing? Why should I watch you? Why should I *pay* to watch you?

Deborah Greenfield is an award-winning performer and choreographer, and director of Rosa Negra Flamenco. Her work has ranged from ballet and modern dance productions to the J.Lo music video, *Ain't it funny?*:

A great dance performance is the result of all the years one has devoted to being a dancer, an artist and a human being. The training, the study of art, music, film, literature, ideas, etc. – i.e. not only the development of one's physical instrument, but also that of one's aesthetic sense, artistic sensibility, imagination, intellect, sense of humour, humanity. When a performance is captivating, it is all of *that* which is also registering with the audience. On a more practical level, it's also about rehearsal, rehearsal, rehearsal, both with the choreographer and also time spent alone with the material.

Jenny Belingy:

My key to a great performance is summed up by a performance I saw recently by the Alvin Ailey American Dance Company. Each piece, from abstract to classical, was thought-provoking, inspiring and unique. So for me a great dance performance should be inspiring, thought-provoking and sometimes transform your life.

John Byrne: What I pick up from each of our dancers is that a great performance isn't just a collection of steps – it begins with knowing what you want to achieve from your performance. What do you want to communicate to your audience through your dance? So my question to *you* is, if you could communicate just one message in your dance career, what would that message be?

Question 2: What is the one thing you have learned which has made a big difference to your career success?

David: To be honest with yourself.

Jacquie: To always make sure I was having fun. Remembering why I danced in the first place. And learning not to take everything too seriously. Keeping these factors in mind allowed me to do my best regardless of what the people on the other side of the audition table were looking for. It also allowed me to free myself up so that if I didn't get the job, the audition was at least enjoyable both for me and, for the most part, the auditioners. And when they saw me the next time, they *remembered* me. I went to an audition for a choreographer who was big at the time, and in front of everyone he singled me out by mentioning a performance he saw me do quite a while back. I always took great care to be clean and accurate in my dancing, always looking like I was having a great time. I was also a quick study and very proficient in a lot of styles, which kept me in demand. And, I was nice and courteous to everyone.

Deborah: Focus, perseverance, dedication, discipline and daring. Daring to do what feels most truthful for me, as opposed to trying to please others. I find that when one gives oneself permission to do one's own, unique thing, others are more likely to be drawn to it. Therefore, one must also develop a certain ability to withstand the naysayers and conformists.

Jenny: To be myself and stop taking on board other people's negative comments, and to stop comparing myself to other people. Also, to remember that when a tutor makes constructive comments, they are trying to help. To maintain a positive attitude at all times.

John: It seems that a positive attitude works both on and offstage – so what can *you* do to maintain your attitude in spite of trials and challenges? Is there one thing that has helped your career or performance so far? If you can identify it, do it some more!

Question 3: What, in your opinion, is the biggest mistake that dancers make when performing or building a career?

David: There are none. Mistakes are good. You learn from mistakes and it makes you a better performer and artist. Mistakes occur in one's training and professional career; this should not be thought of as bad, more like a helping hand to find out what you need to work on and what it will take to move you forwards.

Jacquie: On the career side, taking it all too seriously and personally. If you don't get the job, there are so many factors that have nothing to do with you, so to get wrapped up in the whys/why nots of it all is a waste of time, and nerve-wracking too. Also listening to too many people giving out advice (including myself!). The most important thing, I found, was figuring out what *I* wanted, not what was right for Mary Jane or Susie Q. Learn as much as you can and remember that the *business* in the word 'showbusiness' is what it's all about. Become savvy about the industry you're in: if you can't sing, take singing lessons; if you can't act, take acting lessons. You increase your work opportunities by being versed in more than one discipline. Also, if you are a hip-hop dancer, learn jazz technique, take ballet classes, take modern and tap classes. Be the dancer who gains a reputation for being able to do many dance styles and do them well. That way, you increase the chances of being in demand – especially if you are a quick study and don't ask too many questions about the steps.

Realise that there are fads in the dance business; if you're not 'in' this week you may be 'in' the next. Keep learning and growing, and have other interests outside of the career. Most of all, remember: you are like no other, with a unique voice and expression all your own. Don't ever aspire to be like anyone else – there are others you may admire, and that's a good guiding tool, but always do *you*. And if you don't know who that is, start finding out!

As far as the performing side goes, sometimes dancers are mechanical and lack expression: that goes back to my earlier comment about dancing from the soul. If you aren't sure what the choreography is about, ask the choreographer for a discussion. In addition, figure out what it means to you. What emotions does the music evoke? If it is a piece without music, what feelings does the movement evoke? Dancers have to remember that they are not just dancers but *actors*, where the body is the voice. Speak up!

Deborah: A lack of focus, perseverance, dedication, discipline and commitment. Certainly, as a choreographer I am very allergic to 'flakiness' (a good old LA word). A high-quality career in dance takes enormous amounts of all of the above and, unfortunately these days, fewer and fewer dancers really understand that dance is potentially as high an art form as any other and requires the same level of respect and devotion.

Jenny: Attitude! If you have it, drop it – a casting director will always pick up on it. If you are good, show it through your performance.

John: Since this is a *book* you're reading, you don't have to answer this question out loud ... but being totally honest with yourself, what is the one thing you are doing (or not doing) now that could be holding your career back? What could you do to address this?

Question 4: Has anything gone wrong while you were on stage, and how did you cope?

David: Nothing major has gone wrong, but the obvious 'going blank' has happened and it happens to everyone. I just improvised and picked it back up at the next available point.

Jacquie: So many episodes – which one to choose from? OK, I was dancing in a show on Broadway called *Play On!*, and during an exceptionally fast number called 'Fidgety Feet' I had a costume mishap. The piece was set in the 1930s and we ladies had to wear many layers: tights, bloomers, and then the stockings, held up by a garter belt. (I'm sure many of your readers will have no idea what a garter belt looks like!) Anyway, this particular performance was for Equity Fights Aids in NYC, we played to a full house and many of my colleagues were in attendance. A few shows back, I had been advised by a cast member to wear the garter belt under the bloomers but it would have been a pain, and since I hadn't had any problems I didn't see the need to change. Never a particularly skinny dancer, I felt it would be virtually impossible for the thing to fall down over my ample hips and derrière.

So, the music heats up and I'm facing my partner as we go into this Charleston section – then I feel air. I look down and my garter belt is down around my ankles, still attached to my seafoam stockings … we're about to move into a straight line for this 'chorus line' type kick segment as the music gets even faster. My partner, who is always making us laugh, was absolutely speechless. What's a girl to do? Exit the stage or keep going? Man, I bent down, grabbed that garter belt in the middle and hi-tailed it into the line with my cast mates, kicking my legs up as high as the belt allowed them to go. Needless to say, the dancers on either side of me were in stitches, as well as the audience. It took everything I had not to pass out laughing and to make it all the way off from Stage Left to Stage Right! Just one of many mishaps in my career, all dealing with costumes!

Deborah: Not really, except for the occasional mistake on one's own or somebody else's part. It's important to be comfortable enough on stage – and flexible, inventive – to improvise around a slight mishap if necessary and to avoid telegraphing it to the audience.

Jenny: At a recent performance the finale was chaotic with no particular format or order. The next thing I could see was the theatre ceiling: I'd slipped on something on the stage and come crashing down on my elbow (I can feel the pain all over again!). But in all my pain I kept the smile on my face, and the audience thought it was part of the routine. My disaster-coping technique: keep smiling … at least until you get offstage.

John: Over and over again, clients ask me what to do to prevent something from going wrong onstage. The truth is, if you perform regularly enough, something *will* go wrong once in a while. All you can do is work on the skills you have, so that you know you can cope with it. Make a list of *your* skills and your worst stage fears: is there a skill you could brush up on to make you more confident in dealing with that potential problem?

Question 5: Who is your dance hero or heroine, and why?

David: Matthew Bourne. He has achieved so much and is as real as real can be. He was a normal boy and now he is one of the biggest choreographers around for contemporary and classical dance as well as musical theatre. He takes risks and challenges people's perceptions as well as recreating work for the modern-day audience.

Jacquie: I'd have to say Debbie Allen. When I was out in the field, she had the type of career I wanted to have. She moved seemingly effortlessly from the stage to the small screen to the big one; from a dancer to a singer headlining a show on Broadway, to an actress in film, to a player behind the scenes. At the time when African-American talent was invisible – for actresses, in particular – she seemed to do it all and with such power in her performances. Also impressive because it was so hard for dancers to transition from dancing to being a singing lead and then an actress. And she was my height, short for a dancer nowadays!

Deborah: I don't have any single hero or heroine, but have been influenced and inspired by: Gene Kelly for his enormous vitality; Fred Astaire for his incredible musicianship, imagination, and the nuances of his dancing; Charlie Chaplin for his profoundly human use of body language; Twyla Tharp for her ground-breaking fusion of different dance forms and the funkiness of her vocabulary; William Forsythe of Frankfurt and Mats Ek of Sweden for their ability to breathe new life into the ballet world with their remarkably expressive and contemporary choreography; and finally contemporary flamenco dancers Belen Maya and Eva la Yerbbuena, for the quality of their work as well as their daring to break new ground in a formerly rather rigid tradition.

Jenny: This is really hard; there are so many who have had a huge impact on my life in some shape or form. The main artists have been Gregory Hines, Janet Jackson, Ben Vereen, Josephine Baker and Cyd Charisse, amongst many others. Gregory Hines, well he just had this street style which was effortless, raw. I always wished I could tap dance like that, he wasn't only a great dancer/choreographer but a brilliant actor too. I feel that his contribution to dance/film wasn't recognised enough.

I saw Ben Vereen dance once, but that stuck in my head. It was in the film *Sweet Charity* which starred Shirley MacLaine. It was breathtaking to watch his long legs just gliding across the stage, so gracefully ... a performance I will never forget. And Janet Jackson – what can I say? Slick, effortless, stylish; she puts her all into every single performance and still maintains that energy throughout her live shows. For me, she is one of the best female dancers and stands out a mile in this century, with regards to her street style.

Cyd Charisse had these long legs that went on forever, I saw her in quite a few films with Fred Astaire and Gene Kelly. She was so graceful and when she elevated her leg it looked so easy. Cyd reminded me of a gazelle. As for Josephine Baker, she was a brave woman who persevered in everything she put her mind to.

John: If you admire someone, you normally see qualities in them that are also in you ... or at least the *potential* for those qualities is in you. Make a list of your favourite performers (as you have seen, they don't necessarily have to be dancers). What are the qualities you notice in them? Which of those qualities have you got, if you would only use them?

Question 6: What is your main goal for your future career?

David: The world is my oyster! Ideally I would like to join a company, either in the UK or abroad; but ultimately I would just like to have a successful career in the dance industry whether it is performing, teaching or choreographing.

Jacquie: Now I am on the other side of the table, as a freelance master teacher/choreographer, and I see my future in this – continuing to inspire, guide and train the dancers of tomorrow.

I intend to continue to expand my teaching base: as I write this, I am in Hong Kong working on an international summer dance programme – a great opportunity to work with people in other countries and cultures. This fuels and inspires what I do.

Deborah: To continue to develop as a performer, choreographer and dance filmmaker, with a focus on contemporary, non-tradition-bound flamenco work. Presently I am looking to forge more opportunities for my work to be seen further afield and reach a wider audience.

Jenny and John: As you can see, it doesn't matter how success-ful a working dancer becomes – what keeps them successful is the desire to move forwards and to conquer new worlds. Use your career goal to motivate you to perform to your highest ability onstage, and use this final tip from world-renowned tap dancer Brenda Bufalino to remind you that a performer is only half of a good performance:

Brenda: Remain interested in and committed to your work. Sometimes it may seem that the performance of your work is removed from the work you are doing: that is when the trouble begins. Remain physically, emotionally and spiritually con-nected to every step you are making and the performance takes care of itself. Respect your audience, and realise that they came with the hope that they would love what you do. They are your partner, your intimate. You are letting them in on the secret of your work … you share the gift of attention which raises the moment from the ordinary to the sublime.

Chapter Six

Staying on Your Feet

Health and the working dancer

We have compared dance to sport several times in this book already. Perhaps the most obvious connection between the two is the fact that, as enjoyable as both career paths can be, injuries are commonplace. In most cases these are not too serious, but professionals in both careers have to accept that if serious injury *is* sustained, it can put a premature end to their ability to make a living.

Hopefully even after a long break they can get back in the game, and in some cases even reach new heights of excellence. Tour de France champion Lance Armstrong used his battle against cancer to spur him on to even greater achievements, and dance legend Rudolf Nureyev battled many demons – both mental and physical – to produce critically acclaimed performances. But there are also many tragic tales of sports heroes and dancers who never quite achieved their full potential as a result of early or mid-career injuries.

This leads us to an area in which dancers and sportspeople are *not* quite so similar. As a general observation, it seems to us that while most serious sportspeople are fully aware of the dangers that serious injury can pose to their career and take appropriate precautions as a matter of course, some dancers are not quite so thorough. There are a few extenuating circumstances: for one thing there tends to be a lot more money invested in the success of rising sports stars than in the career of rising dancers. Another key point is that if the sports star is employed by a team, there will usually be a full support staff of coaches, physios and medical personnel to keep an eye on them and deal with any problems that may arise. However, just as you shouldn't wait for an agent or manager to motivate you to reach for excellence in your dance career, so you shouldn't use the fact that nobody else is pushing you to take proper care of your health and wellbeing. It is possible for a singer or an actor with a sore throat to make it through a gig without the audience knowing – or at least without too much loss in performance quality – but a dancer with a painful sprain needs to be really careful about deciding whether or not to perform. For one thing, if the injury is severe enough it will be difficult to display the balance and grace needed to produce the required performance; for another, the very act of dancing with the injury can turn a mild problem into a serious one.

Take heart from the fact that even a serious dance injury may not be the end of one's showbusiness career. James Bond actress Michelle Yeoh, also the action star of movies like *Crouching Tiger, Hidden Dragon*, is a former dancer whose career was cut short by back injury. Some dancers who have had to curtail their performing career because of injury have moved into teaching or some other dance-related area; in doing so they have not only helped and inspired a vast number of other dancers, but also discovered a love of their chosen sphere that even surpasses their love of performance itself. For more information on the options available to the retired or injured dancer, see Chapter Eight.

Nothing we suggest in this chapter can guarantee that your dance career will be disaster-free. But by following a few simple, logical guidelines you can do a lot to avoid injury – or, if the worst happens, to minimise the severity of the problem and its effects on your dancing. *Always* get matters related to your health and wellbeing checked out by a qualified professional.

Avoiding injury

If you have already begun your dance training, you'll know that while dancing certainly requires grace, creativity and the ability to express oneself through visual performance, it also requires tremendous amounts of flexibility, strength and stamina. If you haven't had the experience for yourself, think of some of the dance moves which, while they look impressive, are often taken for granted – like when a male dancer lifts a female dancer high off the ground – and then consider the strain on the muscles which this involves. Or consider the fact that quite often, making a complicated series of dance moves look like they 'come naturally' is something that can only be achieved with long hours of training the body to take on positions and to perform movements that are not necessarily natural at all ... such as dancing on one's toes. Artistic beauty aside, the average dance career is going to put the dancer's body under quite a lot of stress.

For this reason you will certainly ache at the beginning of your dance training – and it is not necessarily a bad thing. At the start of your journey you may find new ways of thinking and new ways of moving difficult to master, even frustrating – but precisely *because* they are new and unfamiliar you will give them your full focus. By contrast, in mid-career it is all too easy to slip into taking things for granted. When John was younger, his father used to work on a metal turning lathe – a lethal piece of equipment if you get in the way of the blade. Thankfully John's dad made it to the end of his career with all ten fingers intact, but quite a few lathe operators haven't been so fortunate. Significantly it is not usually in the early stages of learning to use a lathe that such injuries happen: the new operator is much too wary for that. Ten or 20 years later, though, when using the machine becomes 'second nature', the attention can wander and ... well, we're sure you can imagine the rest.

As an experienced dancer it can be equally tempting to miss stretches or warm-ups just once too often, or to try a move that hasn't been properly prepared. If the body isn't as supple as it should be, one awkward landing can have consequences just as severe for the dancer as a wrong move can have for the lathe operator. Just as you must perform every gig as though it were your first, so you should look after your health and safety at every point in your career.

For the dancer, the most basic injury-prevention technique is simply to be aware of your own body and its strengths and limitations. For instance, if your knee is weak, you need to avoid routines which put undue strain on it. This might seem like very simplistic advice, but it is advice that dancers often ignore. It is understandable to fear being left out in the cold if you reveal your weaknesses, but a good choreographer or teacher will often be able to adjust a routine to compensate for the problem. And when you are dancing in pairs or in a group, if you say nothing about your knee and then it 'goes' at the wrong time, you run the risk of injuring not only yourself but other dancers too. This will certainly go down a lot worse than simply admitting to the problem in the first place.

It goes without saying that if you are pregnant or have a heart condition, you need to let the choreographer or teacher know. Again, you may be surprised by how accommodating they can be – but they are not mind-readers. It also follows that if they do advise you to sit out certain moves, they know what they are talking about and you would do well to take their advice. One missed class, or taking a backseat for a particular routine, is a lot less frustrating than putting yourself out of action for weeks or even months. If you dance regularly with a partner then you owe it to each other to be open about any health or injury issues that you may have (see also pp. 110–11 on the partnership relationship) – after all, *your* ability to work directly affects *their* ability to work.

Another basic safety rule is to pay attention to the condition of the areas you are dancing in. Not every dance class, stage or studio is of Hollywood standards. A break in the floor-covering or a slippery stairway may not seem very dangerous, but catch your toe in it while performing a high-kick or lose your balance while rushing to class, and the results can be very unpleasant. A proper insurance policy should be a priority both for you and for the people who teach or employ you.

Warming up and stretching before dancing is vitally important, but cooling down afterwards is equally so. Busy dancers running from class to class or from gig to gig often neglect the cool-down – big mistake! Rest is important, too: injuries and poor dance technique often occur when you try to learn something new in an overtired state. In fact, injuries and tiredness often go hand-in-hand.

The better you learn to dance, the less chance you have of injuring yourself. Good posture and good technique mean that you are using your body safely ... so it follows that bad technique is going to put even more stress on your bones and joints than is necessary. Keep doing something the wrong way, and you greatly increase your chances of injury: it has been estimated that about a third of most reported injuries are associated with overuse, and 80 per cent of those injuries occur in the knee, ankle or foot.

No matter how careful you are, you are going to experience pain at some point in your dance career. This is not to say that you should collapse in a heap at every little twinge, but since pain is a signal from your body that something needs looking at, it is not wise to simply ignore it. Pain which persists or recurs for more than a day or two is always worth checking out: better a 'wasted' medical examination than an expensive medical procedure further down the line because something serious has been missed.

It would take a whole book to list all the ways in which dancers can injure themselves – and somewhere, even as we write, there are probably dancers inventing new ones! The following are some of the most common, but remember that they are offered as a guide: *always* consult a professional for a proper diagnosis.

Common foot and ankle problems among dancers

1 **Affecting the toes:**
   a) Corns/soft corns/callus – partly covering the arch
   b) Bunion or hallux/hallux valgus/hallux rigidus/bunionette/ tailor's bunion
   c) Morton's neuroma/hammertoes/claw toe/ingrown toenail/ arthritis (often affects dancers in later life)

2 **Affecting the mid-section of the foot:**
   a) Tendon problems/blood vessels
   b) Muscle strain/arthritis
   c) Arch problems

3 **Affecting the heel:**
   a) Tendon problems/Achilles tendon problems
   b) Ankle sprain/ankle instability/tibial tendonitis or rupture
   c) Arthritis/plantar fasciitis (heel spur)

Other common ailments include curved or sickle feet, knee pains, and muscle strain in the feet, legs, thighs and lower back.

Treating the problem

Although pharmacists can prescribe remedies for some of the more minor ailments listed above, a podiatrist or foot specialist should be a regular stop-off point on your journey to fame, even if you don't have any immediate need for help. If you are in a good school, or professional company or show, they may refer you to an appropriate specialist; if you are independent, there is still a lot to be said for calling one of these organisations and asking whom they normally send people to.

If you do take a problem to a medical professional, their first step will be to find out as much information as possible. You'll be asked obvious questions like where and when does it hurt? How long has the pain been going on? And some possibly less obvious, but nevertheless very relevant, questions like: What kind of shoes were you wearing when the problem first occurred? They may also arrange for you to have X-rays or some other type of scan done. Obviously, the more experienced the specialist is with performers in general, and with dancers in particular, the better the questions they can ask – and the more observant you have been, the more helpful the answers you will be able to give. There is certainly nothing to be gained by not being honest about the discomfort you are in. Dancers have a habit of down-playing pain for fear it might mean taking time off performing, or even worse. However, this is a surefire way of making certain that even minor ailments turn into bad news. As frustrating as an enforced break from dancing can be, it is worth resting and doing whatever exercises the experts recommend to ensure that when you do return to dance, you return for good. Going back too quickly, and then having to crash out again because you have overdone it on a weak joint or muscle, is going to affect your professional reputation a lot worse than if you simply take the time out to heal properly.

Health, fitness – and weighty issues

It makes absolutely no sense to take care of the dance-specific aspects of your health and safety if you don't look after your general wellbeing too. This *should* stand to reason – but just as many singers, being totally dependent on their voices to make a living, seem to be hell-bent on destroying that very instrument by smoking, so we have come across our fair share of dancers who seem determined to treat their bodies in exactly the same way.

Looking after your body means looking ahead, too. A musician who hears a 'bum note' from his keyboard, or who finds her composing software crashing once too often, is going to take the offending equipment for a service sooner rather than later. Aside from the fact that big problems which are expensive to solve usually start off as smaller problems that could have been caught early without too much trouble, the last thing the performer wants is to have their equipment fail just as they have an important gig coming up. The serious dancer needs to develop the same foresight, health-wise. Most of us can afford to wait out a few sniffles to see if they are a mild cold or full-blown flu, but performers, knowing that a serious bout of flu can take them out of the running for lucrative tours or important auditions, will queue up for their flu jab each winter alongside the senior citizens. This is not being 'precious'; it's a sensible precaution.

The dancer disregards their health and appearance at their peril – but there is a 'flipside' to this, too. As the whole world becomes more and more concerned with image, it follows that this preoccupation will be even more prevalent in the world of showbusiness. Dance is one of the professions most prone to insecurity about physique, and we have heard some terrible tales of misery, particularly related to weight and eating habits, as a result. While the majority of dance teachers and mentors are highly committed, qualified and sensible, not all the misinformation that abounds in the profession comes from beginners. One performer was told by a drama teacher that 'black girls' bones are too heavy for them to be ballerinas' – a notion that managed to combine racism with complete rubbish, yet unsurprisingly triggered years of insecurity for the performer about her size. And of course every dance community is rife with the latest diets, from the faddy to the downright dangerous: sadly, bulimia and anorexia are not unfamiliar phenomena to anyone who has spent much time backstage. Contrary to popular belief, such issues and anxieties are common to male dancers as much as to female ones, although men may not talk about them as much.

So let's separate fact from fiction. Yes, mainstream dancers are required to meet certain specifications in terms of size and appearance limits – though there are, of course, agencies and sometimes entire dance troupes which specialise in performers who are *not* the usual size. In fact some of the most lucrative advertising jobs go to just such performers. The thing to remember is that those specifications are a lot broader than most people suppose. Regardless of how bulky or skinny you are, how tall or petite, or how long your legs or rounded your behind, what counts is how hard you are prepared to make the best of whatever attributes God has given you. For everyone who squeezes into an uplift bra to make her chest appear larger, there is someone else choosing a loose flowing top to make her breasts look smaller. And the truth is that for both dancers there are jobs that will suit one build more than the other.

Just as we shouldn't compare our own dance style too closely to someone else's, our best friend's health regime may not be the right one for us. If you are one of those fortunate people who can knock back junk food with no apparent weight change, good for you – although whether or not the food affects your waistline, it is probably not going to make your skin look very pretty. For the rest of us, keeping an eye on what we eat should do the trick. With a little observation it's not too difficult to identify the foods that pile on the weight in our particular case. Of course, these are usually the foods we most enjoy: a sad fact of life! Saying that we're going to eat well is one thing – but for the professional dancer, *doing* it can be a bit more difficult. The nature of showbusiness life is that it involves a lot of stopping and starting, working strange hours and living out of a suitcase, so that proper food is not always as accessible as the snack machine. Finances too can limit the choices available to the dancer starting out. But try to make sure you get at least one decent meal a day. Expert advice can really help here: contrary to what fast-food manufacturers would love you to believe, it is perfectly possible to eat cheaply, well *and* healthily if you know how. Self-invented 'diets', on the other hand, are almost always useless at best or dangerous at worst.

If you do find yourself worrying about your weight more than normal, and in particular if you feel that you might be suffering from bulimia or another food disorder, it is important that you seek help sooner rather than later. Anyone who has worked in showbusiness for any length of time, in any capacity, knows that far from being a non-stop whirl of excitement and glamour, it can sometimes be a very lonely place – particularly so if we have problems or concerns we feel we can't share with our fellow performers in case we might 'ruin our image'. If you feel that you have nobody to talk to, there are several organisations listed in our resource section that you could contact: even if you never need them yourself – and we sincerely hope you don't – you might be the dancer who reaches out to a colleague or even a rival just when they need help the most.

One advantage a dancer has over other types of performer is that if you are dancing or even just training with some degree of regularity, your general fitness level should be above average. Some dancers like to go the extra mile and make a really good physique one of their selling points. If this appeals to you, whether you can afford ongoing fitness training or not it might be a good investment to book an assessment at the local gym, where you can have a proper training programme mapped out for you based on the goals that you want to achieve. Many gyms offer off-peak membership and this can suit entertainers; our hours are different from everyone else's, anyhow.

If you can't afford a personal trainer, a training buddy is the next best thing – all you need is a friend who is equally committed to working-out as you are. The ideal training buddy is someone who'll tell you off if you slack off or don't show up. After all, that's basically what you'd be paying a personal trainer to do. Another good investment would be to have a session with a nutritionist: as we've already noted, the potential for dancers to miss meals and eat junk is far greater than for many other professionals. Get proper advice on which vitamins and supplements to take. Your average health shop has a huge array of concoctions, all promising amazing benefits: some of these products can be very good, compensating for missed meals, late nights and general physical and mental wear and tear, but others are a complete waste of money and may possibly do you more harm than good. Bear in mind that dancers need to take special care of their joints, not just for the benefit of their current career but also to avoid problems in the future. Again, there is a wide range of supplements available to aid joint health. Seek medical opinion on which one is best for you, and when you do find it, we encourage you to take it ... your joints will thank you for it in later life!

There is of course one way in which you can 'improve' your body without recourse to exercise or diet, and that's in the murky area of cosmetic surgery. It's not for us to tell you how to spend your money: indeed there are certain kinds of cosmetic surgery, such as getting your teeth fixed if they are not in great shape, that we'd heartily approve of. However, don't use 'furthering your career' as an excuse to amplify existing doubts about your self-image. The big danger with cosmetic surgery is that it might just change your physical appearance while leaving the underlying doubts unaddressed. And it's those doubts that will hold your career back, far more drastically than any perceived problems with your physical appearance.

Mental health

One of the reasons dancers tend to do really well when they eventually leave the stage is that they need to develop a certain degree of resilience to make it in the performing world. Ego plays a part in virtually every kind of showbusiness endeavour, but there are some jobs, such as singing or acting, where the 'inner diva' is not just tolerated but may well be encouraged. We're not suggesting that you won't find your fair share of prima donnas – male and female – in the dance world too, but in general dancers tend to have slightly more reason to keep their egos in check. For one thing, dancers – particularly at the beginning of their careers – usually have to work in groups, which means that some kind of team spirit has to develop. If one person looks bad, the whole group looks bad. For another, as we have already noted, a lot of dance work involves supporting someone else's act. Standing out is not necessarily the route to further bookings.

Unfortunately, the downside of developing these qualities – being a team player, sharing the spotlight, and making strenuous physical activity look easy and graceful – is that not everyone in the business (including producers and directors who should know better) gives dancers the respect they deserve. While we have done our best to give you some tools to help you cope with the auditioning process (see Chapter Four), there is no getting away from the fact that the selection methods used can be very unpleasant. A few minutes in which to show your stuff, and then instant dismissal if you don't make the cut – it's an ordeal that certainly requires a thick skin to put up with on a regular basis. But it's also a pretty good taster of people's general attitude to dancers within the business. If one of the singers in a show can't perform for whatever reason, an understudy may well be found but the place will usually be kept open for the original artist if there's a chance that they can come back. However, if a *dancer* twists an ankle or has to drop out for any other reason ... well, there are a lot more dancers ready, willing and able to take the place. And very few people in the audience would even notice.

There are organisations which work hard to promote the rights of dancers (you'll find some of them in our resource section), but the general lack of respect that dancers often have to put up with is probably not going to change overnight. Your job is not to let that attitude change how you feel about your work – and even more important, how you feel about you. The strength of character you develop while working your way up as a dancer can be a very useful attribute. Just be careful that it doesn't harden into bitterness or cynicism, the two main causes of failure in most showbusiness careers.

However hard you try to keep your spirits up, there are bound to be days when you feel like giving up and that all your efforts are for nothing. These days can be especially frequent when you have long periods between dance jobs. Because dancers are physical performers, they have a lot of energy pent up waiting for release. If it is not released in a working environment then it can channel itself into less useful, or even dangerous, pursuits. Most addictions, whether they be to sex, drugs or rock-and-roll, are not about the addictive substance or activity itself but about a desire to escape from a particular situation. Unfortunately, addictions can be more difficult to escape from than the situation you were trying to get away from in the first place. Here are some tips for keeping 'resting' performers sane and optimistic. We can't promise that they will make your non-dancing days fun – but they will certainly make them more bearable.

1 *Prioritise.* Rather than setting yourself huge goals and beating yourself up because you are not reaching them, it's much better to acknowledge that while you're feeling down, you

may not get everything done. So start each day by listing everything you need to do and then choose the one or two tasks that will make the most difference to your career. Do those tasks first if you can – but whatever else you don't get round to, make sure that at least those valuable tasks get addressed.

2 *Watch the company you keep.* That's not to suggest you drop any friends who may also be out-of-work performers; between jobs we are all out-of-work performers. And it is certainly hard for anyone outside the profession to fully empathise with the frustration of feeling that your talent is unrecognised. But empathy and a 'pity party' are two very different things. If you are telling yourself that you may never work again, you certainly don't need a Greek chorus of colleagues agreeing with you. Seek out people who are optimistic (not naïve) and active (not desperate), and work on keeping each other's spirits up.

3 *Exercise.* When you are out of work, it may seem that keeping fit is a waste of time – but this is exactly when looking after yourself is most important. You do not have to join an expensive gym or studio if money is tight: a regular walk or taking up a sport will do just as well, or a local dance class might suit you better. Besides its physical benefits, exercise lifts the spirits and breaks you out of your rut ... and that is what you most need right now.

4 *Accentuate the positive.* Keep a list of your successes, no matter how small. A successful audition that leads to a job offer is great, but any positive comment or feedback even when you did not get the part are indicators that you're doing something right. Taking five minutes each night to fill in a 'gratitude journal' might sound silly, but it works for me and for most people I have suggested it to. The underlying principle, which almost every performer will understand, is that you always get more of what you focus on, so it is better to focus on success. It's no secret that many of the dancers who do stay focused and successful have a spiritual dimension to their lives; a belief that there's something bigger than them which prevents them from getting caught up either in self-doubt or in self-importance.

Whether or not you have 'someone up there' to talk to, it makes sound sense to have a good team around you down here. Friends or family, hairdressers or sound engineers, even other dancers you've become friends with – you need to surround yourself with people who like you for *you*, not because of your image or the successes you have enjoyed. A good team will tell you the whole truth: that means helping you identify things you do which work, so you can do more of them, as well as areas that need improvement so you can get busy improving them.

Even with a good team around you, you need to keep your own focus and a clear head. Over the course of your career you'll be offered lots of advice: some will be well-meaning, some not; some will come from friends and family, some from fans, some from experts, some from other performers and some from books like this one. Ultimately, you are the only person who can decide which advice is going to work to your benefit. Just as knowing your body is the best way to maintain your physical health, so the best way to maintain mental stability is to know your own mind.

Safety

An important part of looking after your health and welfare as a dancer is taking sensible and appropriate precautions to ensure your personal safety. Particularly at the beginning of your career you will find yourself travelling alone to venues you've never been to, often coming home late at night or, if you're on tour, staying in cheap guest houses or hotels. The 'glamour' of showbusiness can work its magic even in the smallest, dingiest pub – but unfortunately, sometimes this 'magic' can attract undesirable attention from audience members who don't understand that once the show is over, you have a right to your privacy and personal space.

Obviously personal safety is a particular issue for the female dancer, but it's not unknown for male dancers to attract unwelcome attention too – whether of the unwanted romantic kind, or more usually from the large bloke who has decided that his wife or girlfriend fancies you and wants to beat you up. In an ideal world you won't be going to gigs alone, of course, but even the most dedicated spouse, partner or circle of friends may not be available 24/7. So, male or female, it makes sense to apply 'blind date' safety principles to your dancing gigs.

1 If you're going to a venue for the first time, check the address beforehand and make sure you let someone know where you're performing.

2 Take a mobile phone and make sure that you have a local cab number (yes, the venue management should sort this out for you, but you still need to have a 'plan B'). Given the huge fluctuation in the quality of promoters and venues up and down the country, it does no harm to keep an eye on fire exits and the state of microphone leads and other electrical appliances that are on stage when you are. Have a good look at the stage you are dancing on: if you can't get any major holes covered (do try!) before you go on, at least you'll know where they are.

3 Even at the lower end of the showbiz ladder, anyone on stage is assumed to have money. Don't make it easy for thieves to relieve you of yours. Don't take any valuables with you that you don't need for your show, and make sure there's somewhere *secure* in the venue to leave them while you're on stage. Often this does *not* mean the dressing room. Be particularly careful about leaving any stage costumes or props unattended.

4 As far as is possible, aim to leave the venue as soon as you've finished the gig (and been paid, of course). Besides being safer, this makes you look more like a star! If you have a business card or website address you can give it out as a contact for anyone who wants to talk to you after the performance (make sure your home address isn't on anything you're handing out freely). If someone really is serious about offering you work, they'll hang on to the number and contact you. If the gig has gone well you may find that punters want to buy you drinks: it's up to you whether you accept them, but make sure the combination of excitement and alcohol doesn't end up drowning your common sense.

It wouldn't be thorough to close a chapter on safety without a word about sexual health. Showbusiness and casual sexual relations have a reputation for going hand-in-hand (although if it stopped at hand-in-hand, fewer people would get into trouble!). And deservedly or otherwise, dancers sometimes have a reputation for being at best highly sexed, and at worst 'easy'. Actually there are as many different attitudes to sex as there are dancers, and someone whose image is highly sexual in performance can be far more reserved offstage.

While sexual activity can sometimes be seen as a means of career advancement, sexually transmitted diseases are definitely bad for the career – and sex in exchange for a 'big break' is a very unsafe transaction. In most cases the big break doesn't materialise once you have given what was wanted, and even if it does, showbusiness is a very small world. If your career vision involves maintaining any kind of reputation as a talented dancer, developing a name for being 'loose' certainly isn't going to help you. There will always be someone around who is younger and prettier, but if you focus on getting your work by virtue of talent and your uniqueness, nobody else will be able to surpass you.

Chapter Seven

There's No Business Like Toe Business

Business skills for the working dancer

We hope it's clear from the general tone of this book that we love the world of showbusiness. What could be better than doing something you love all day and getting paid for it? However, in order to *keep* getting paid for it, you have to run your dance business just as professionally as you would any other business – something that performers as a whole don't pay as much attention to as they should. Take your eye off the 'business ball' long enough, and your career can come to a grinding halt. More to the point, if you don't pay enough attention to the management of both your talent and your money, there are a lot of other people out there who may be a lot quicker to take advantage of both. Not everyone you will come across in showbusiness is a shark or a charlatan – that's as much of a cliché as the notion that everything is sweetness and light – but there are enough of these people about that if you don't keep your wits about you, you are liable to get badly bitten.

Once you're out on stage, your success or failure is generally down to you, your talent and how you relate to your audience. But getting on to that stage, and what happens when you come off it, involves you in a whole range of business activity – much of which is completely unrelated to performing. It's not possible to cover all this in detail in one chapter or even in a whole book ... but we can bring some of the key issues to your attention here and hope that you will find out more about them through practice, experience and further reading. It's worth pointing out here that although there are people in the dance business who will take advantage of you, plenty of performers don't *need* any help getting shafted: they are perfectly capable of shooting themselves in the foot. Their passion for dance and joy in performing can be all-consuming; certainly far more attractive than more mundane activities like balancing cheque books, filing receipts or going to meetings with the bank manager. Yet contrary to popular belief, people who are naturally gifted creatively and in performance *can* and *do* manage a business. Let us cast aside the myth that there's anything mysterious or difficult about successful business practice, or that dancers are any less qualified to do it than anyone else. You may need some professional help and advice, but in the end it is essential for you to retain a good understanding and firm control of the business side of your dance career.

As with marketing your talents (see Chapter Three), you may want to farm out the bits of business that you don't enjoy to someone who can do them better. However, you need to know what you're asking them to do first so you can stay in control and make sure they do it. There are plenty of managers, agents and accountants who operate with absolute honesty and integrity – but there are also performers who use the 'I'm not good at business' excuse when they actually mean 'I'm too lazy to learn about business'. Sadly it's this latter type of performer who tends to fall into the clutches of the many showbiz hangers-on who are ready, willing and able to take them for a ride. They will convince you that you really need their services to further your career; then they will take a percentage of your earnings and/or your self-esteem in exchange for doing something that you could do perfectly well yourself. Showbusiness is no different from any other business: the same basic principles apply. Take some time to learn these, and they will stand you in good stead throughout your dance career – and beyond.

Finances

'I don't care about the money, I'm in it for my art' is a common cry of dancers, actors, singers and creative talents of all types. Unfortunately, a chronic lack of money is the reason the vast majority of performers are unable to pursue their career at the level they would like. Yes, there *are* fortunes to be made in showbusiness and, despite what we've written above, dancers do make them, too. Equally there are a lot of dancers living precariously from gig to gig, or working in energy-sapping part-

or full-time jobs to earn enough for them to work on their dancing. There's nothing wrong with temping to fund your dance career; if you don't have to at some point, you're the exception, not the rule. The important thing – especially at the beginning of your career – is not *how much* money is coming into the business but how well you *manage* that money.

Recent surveys have thrown up frightening statistics about how badly the average member of the public manages their money, with levels of poverty and debt rising all the time. The performer's mentality lends itself especially well to flamboyant overspending even when there is no money to spend – and things are not made easier by the existence of easy credit and aggressive consumer advertising. For showpeople there's a further temptation: the fact that no matter how badly we manage our money, there's always the hope that just around the corner will come the 'big break', the gig where we are discovered, the West End contract, the tour with Beyonce that will end our money worries for ever. Of course, it might happen (and if it does, please mention this book in all your TV interviews!), but trading on the possibility of good luck tomorrow, rather than managing your money sensibly today, is the road to ruin. Moreover, many people who have enjoyed that big break, big contract and big hit tour have gone on to prove that if you can't handle money when you have a little of it, you will mess things up on an even more spectacular level when you get a lot of it.

Step number one in managing your finances is to 'bite the bullet' and see where you actually are financially. This is particularly important if there are a large number of unopened brown envelopes piling up on the carpet. Take a deep breath and open them. Make a list of everything you owe and everything that is coming in regularly, whether from your day job or from your dancing. (If you don't have a regular income, figure out a monthly estimate.) Now subtract your monthly outgoings total from your monthly income and you are left with your disposable income. This is the money you have available to invest in enjoying youself or in furthering your career.

What if you don't have any money left – or worse, end up with a large minus figure? Thanks to the wonders of high-interest credit cards and other 'easy' loans, it is now perfectly possible for performers – a species once ranked somewhere between kamikaze pilots and bomb disposal crews as poor credit risks – to get access to more borrowed money than is good for them. And thanks to the average performer's capacity to live life in the fast lane, it is equally possible to get into a huge amount of debt extremely quickly. If this is the case, take heart: the first step in dealing with a problem is to recognise it. The next step is to get things sorted out as soon as you possibly can. It is very difficult to carry yourself like the major star that you are if you have to step over a mountain of unopened bills every time you step outside your door. There are now several charities dealing with debt management; they will help you work out a budget and negotiate a repayment scheme with your creditors. Try these organisations first in preference to commercial debt-management companies who perform exactly the same function but charge you for the privilege, thereby increasing rather than decreasing your debt. Cut down too on all but essential spending, but that *doesn't* mean compromising on your performance style. Start home cooking with simple ingredients, and it's amazing how soon the money saved from all those takeway meals mounts up enough to cover a new backing track or getting your stage outfits dry-cleaned.

Even if you do have money coming in from dance jobs or other employment and aren't up against the wall financially, good money management is a useful habit to acquire. For one thing, entertainment income by its nature fluctuates considerably – so even with a run of well-paid gigs, it's a good idea to put something aside for drier periods. You'll also need to put something aside for tax, because whether your dance income is earned full-time or as an 'extra', it's all taxable and you need to declare it – not least because the venues and companies employing you will be declaring it when they do their end-of-year accounts. The Inland Revenue is very strict about tax returns and will hold out for every penny you owe, not to mention charge high rates of interest if you fall behind.

If accounts really aren't your strong point (and even if they are), the time and grief you can save by hiring an accountant to make your tax returns may more than justify the cost (and like a lot of your showbusiness expenditure, you can claim for that). If you do get an accountant it pays to get one who knows showbusiness. Since a dancer's income tends to be sporadic, a good accountant may be able to (legally) spread payments over two years to make things a bit less painful. However, having an accountant is no excuse for not keeping an overview of your own financial affairs. Quite a lot of the high-profile financial disasters that have befallen well-known performers have not been so much due to them losing money as not keeping an eye on their money in the first place. If you are computer-minded there are software packages which will do your sums for you ... and even if you use an accountant, the more work you can do, the less you will be charged.

Contracts

We could write a whole book on the ins-and-outs of show-business contracts; indeed, some showbusiness contracts are very nearly long enough to fill up a book all by themselves. No matter how long or short a contract, though, there is one cardinal rule: *never sign any contract or agreement unless you understand exactly what you are signing*. And even then, don't sign it until you've got professional advice. And after you've sought professional advice, leave it in a drawer for a few days until you can look at it with a clear head.

The simple fact is that any contract offered to you or to your agent by a management company, theatre company or a promoter is designed to protect *their* interests, so you need to have it checked out by someone who can protect *yours*. If you have an agent you trust to do this, great – but double-checking it yourself does no harm either. Just as an ordinary GP may be the wrong person to take your dance-related problems to, so the average high-street lawyer may not be equipped to deal with the ins-and-outs of show contracts. No matter how tight money is, running the contract past a qualified showbusiness lawyer is an investment you'll be glad you made. (Under no circumstances use a lawyer recommended by the company you are negotiating with. Yes, we once thought we'd never have to offer such obvious advice, too.)

Never feel shy about asking or checking anything you don't fully understand, and never fall into the trap of thinking that because a contract is described as 'standard', it is not worth checking every term and condition.

If and when you do get a lawyer or an agent to look over your contract, make sure you have a contract, or at least a letter of agreement, with them too. Basically, you need to get into the habit of putting every relationship you have in writing. This may seem a million miles away from the business of dance, but you need to cover all eventualities. Your dancing career will go a lot more smoothly if you have taken pains to ensure that all your business associates are working to its advantage.

Dance partners

There are certain kinds of dance which naturally lead to you working with a partner: ballroom or salsa, for instance. But even if such styles are not in your repertoire, at some time in your career you are likely to work with other dancers, be this in a dance company, a small dance group or as part of the cast of a large show. It follows therefore that people skills play a very important role in building a dance career. This is especially true if you have a closer dance relationship with one or more performers – you have a permanent partner, for example, or are part of a group or collective.

Sometimes these partnerships happen naturally, maybe even starting at college; sometimes they are manufactured – a dance teacher or choreographer may spot that two dancers would make a very good pairing. There's no doubt that a great dance team can achieve heights that the individual dancers may not be able to reach on their own: think about Fred Astaire and Ginger Rogers, for example. But there's another side to partnership, as shown by this letter from John's agony column in *The Stage* newspaper:

> *I am one half of a performing team – or at least I was until last year. My partner and I have been together for about five years but our last show together didn't do very well. I assumed that we would regroup and start again, but in fact I haven't heard from my partner since. I have tried making contact by various means but the response hasn't been very positive. Not only that, but it seems like my 'other half' is moving ahead with their own career while I am left feeling betrayed, hurt and resentful, which is not*

making it any easier to focus on my own work. I am not a confrontational person but I don't like bad feeling either. I genuinely tried to make our act work and I feel I am being treated very unfairly. At this point I am not sure we could ever work together again, but surely things don't have to end this badly – it's not like we were married, but it is certainly feeling like a very painful divorce. How can I make things better and move on?

This story is a very common one, and performing partnerships certainly have a lot in common with marriage: when they work well, both partners have an almost instinctive understanding of how to support each other ... and when they fall apart the rifts may never heal. Add business pressures and egos to the mix and the situation gets even more volatile. Much the same applies to groups who work together, and it is not uncommon for a promoter to try to book a dance group that has played success-fully at his or her venue previously, only to find that there are now two dance groups performing under very similar names.

If you are already in a successful dance partnership, you may find it hard to imagine that a break-up as acrimonious as the one described above could ever occur – and if everyone involved has the same attitude of commitment, positive thinking and business sense advocated throughout this book, there's no reason why it should. But in the real world, people do fall out or simply develop their careers in different directions. So, just as you would with a more formal business arrangement, always make sure that all members of a partnership have agreed *in writing* what the joint responsibilities are, how the money is split and who looks after it, and what will happen to money or outstanding contracts if the couple or group should split up. It can be a pain and an embarrassment to have this kind of discussion at the beginning of a partnership – but it's nothing to the pain and embarrassment that can ensue if the partnership or group breaks up without such issues being sorted out.

Chapter Eight

On With The Dance ...

What to do afterwards

Keeping on top of your art, keeping the business side going and keeping an eye on your health and fitness will certainly prolong your dance career for as long as possible, and give you the best chance of keeping it on an upward path. But in truth there will come a time when the physical side of dancing is not as easy as it once was, and whether by choice or necessity you will start to look at other career avenues besides performing. This happens at different times in dancers' careers and affects them in different ways – but it would certainly seem sensible to begin thinking about these possibilities before it is necessary, rather then hanging on until the last possible moment. The very fact that you are reading this 'how to' book is a good sign; it shows that you are prepared to explore new directions and seek as much extra information as you can to help you achieve your goals. That attitude will not only help you to make your dance career successful, but also stand you in good stead after your dancing days are done.

Ideally, most ex-dancers would like to continue in the profession in some way – perhaps in dance teaching or choreography (see pp. 115–6). However, many of the qualities you have acquired in your dance career will also be very useful, no matter what future career path you take. Throughout this book we have tried to keep one eye on the future and to keep you prepared in some way for the end of the regular performance side of your career. Despite the precautions set out in our health and safety chapter, life can sometimes throw you a curve-ball and injury end your dancing career much earlier then you had planned or wished for. Aside from the practical problems that this may cause, such a disaster can also be a psychological shock to the system – giving you a sense that the dreams which you have worked so hard to achieve have suddenly been snatched away. In fact, even if you have been planning for retirement or down-scaling your performance work, there can still be a sense of regret. After all, you got into dance because you loved dancing, and it is very frustrating when the body no longer has the same ability to push itself as far as the mind would like.

But even if your dance career does come to a premature end, or even if you have just been too focused on the present to make plans for your career after full-time dancing, it is never too late to strike out in new directions. Many of the ex-dancers we know would love to have had a few extra dancing years – but most of them are also happy, healthy and fulfilled ... and in some cases, their post-dance careers have been even more successful than their dancing ones.

The first thing to do when you give up dancing is to realise and accept that there may well be a period of transition. In fact, it may even feel like a period of grieving. If you have ever danced in a long-running tour or show, this feeling is not dissimilar to those experienced on closing night (except that after closing night, you would normally be beginning the audition process again with the hope of securing a new gig or show). Bear in mind that after your last dance gig, it can take weeks or even months for any 'withdrawal symptoms' to kick in. When they do, the first step in coping with them is to actually allow yourself to feel them. A positive attitude is certainly to be encouraged, but equally most of us would admit to some feelings of apprehension too, when moving into the unknown after doing something we have enjoyed for so long.

Many performers – not just dancers – tend to throw themselves into a flurry of activity as soon as their last show finishes, basically as a means of filling the gap. They launch this project and that project with no great direction in mind beyond simply having something to do. On the other hand there are performers who take to their beds, or at least to the sofa in the living room; they are the ones for whom 'performance is life', to the extent that when they are not performing they feel completely useless. Both these responses are about suppressing feelings, either through distraction or withdrawal, and both only serve to make the feelings they are trying to suppress all the stronger. If they are traits you recognise in yourself, it is a good idea to give yourself permission to feel your feelings ahead of time.

That isn't the same thing as being ruled by your feelings, though. If you are naturally prone to insecurity (and many performers are), you may tend to focus on the challenges of making a career transition ('I'm too old to learn new skills now'; 'All I know how to do is dance', etc.) rather than on the positive points. Making a conscious effort to focus on those positives is very important – but what are they?

In general ex-dancers, even injured ones, tend to be fitter than the average person, which is certainly an advantage for employers. Along with health and fitness, poise and personal grooming should be an ingrained habit and there is a wide range of jobs, from customer service to health and fashion, where these qualities are very desirable.

Having to pick up dance steps and routines quickly, and often at short notice, gives the dancer a lot of practice in fast learning – something that employers are particularly keen on. In addition, the basic ability to be at ease and perform well in public (no matter how shy we might be in real life) is a definite plus when it comes to jobs which involve presentation or sales, and the PR industry is certainly one in which ex-dancers can do well. If you are currently or will shortly be dancing as part of a promotional event, it is worth keeping an eye on the other people working on the gig or shoot to see what jobs they do, and asking yourself if they are jobs you might be good at.

And of course the determination it takes to make it as a dancer will certainly give you a head start when working in high-pressure industries where more sensitive souls may not be able to 'cut it'.

These are just a few of the traits which dancers may find useful when changing career. However, long before you arrive at that point we would encourage you to keep track of your own unique areas of strength and experience, as they may well direct your career plan and help you stand out in the jobs market. While we would like to have the space here to list every potential career for the ex-dancer (and through the years we have come across dancers doing very well in almost all of them), space limits us to the main dance-related areas that most people set their sights on. In the resource section of this book you will find several organisations and courses listed which will help you make the most of your career both before and after you give up performing.

Dance teacher

You don't necessarily have to wait for the end of your own dance career to become a dance teacher. In fact, this can be a really good way to finance your career when you are not working on paid gigs. But as you get older, what you may lack in agility and stamina you can certainly make up for in experience – and this experience can be very useful to students and other aspiring performers.

Dance teaching is not a 'rest'; you will have to demonstrate skills and techniques to your students perhaps in several back-to-back classes. Also, while not every good dance teacher is somebody who has natural teaching talent, you do have to have *some* interest in educating people. Almost anyone who has taken a teaching job purely for the money will agree that this in itself isn't enough to make up for the grief! If you've ever been taught by a teacher who was only in it for the money then you'll know that the misery is two-sided.

There are dance teaching posts to be had at every level, from an evening class at your local community centre to a professional dance studio to a top college. Obviously the levels you can teach at, and the money you make, depend on your qualifications. If you do start to see dance teaching as a future path, it might be worth considering some extra study to build up your qualifications.

While many teachers are content to earn their living in established teaching jobs and venues, there are some dancers who prefer to set up their own schools and studios. For such a venture, business skills are as important as and possibly even more important than dance ability. In fact you will probably find yourself hiring others to do the dancing as you focus on marketing, insurance and other headaches – but by this route you can create a successful and maybe even global business. Even if this is your ultimate goal, it might be a good idea to teach in someone else's school for a while to get an idea of how these establishments are run. (Beware of the all-too-frequent practice of 'student poaching' when you start your own academy!)

Choreographer

Choreographers work out dance moves and put them together to form pleasing and exciting routines either for their own sake or as scenes in shows or music videos. The gifts that make a good choreographer include being able to translate ideas into visuals and, as dancers, the ability to motivate and create team spirit and to think of dance in terms of an overall effect – not just their own part in it.

Choreographers working on bigger shows are often on the lookout for dancers who have these qualities so that they can allocate them leadership roles – perhaps taking a team of dancers through some moves they have missed, or even taking charge of an extra rehearsal that the choreographer can't attend. If you are one of those dancers you may graduate to working as an assistant choreographer and eventually to doing the job in your own right.

If this job appeals to you, either as a natural development of your ongoing career or as something to step into at the latter end of it, try to observe closely any choreographers you work with. Try to get an idea of why they design routines as they do, and think about how you would create the routines if you were in charge. Again, there are formal training courses to help you step into this career path, and resources to help you at the back of this book.

Other areas

From dance studios to dance productions, from agencies to make-up and costume specialists, there are many more people involved in the dance world than the dancers themselves. However, if you have a dance background it will certainly help you get in, and make a living. Some of those non-dance skills that we spoke about earlier may well help you find other areas of employment in the dance industry. For instance, being naturally organised may make you an ideal bookings agent for an outfit representing dancers. And Jenny certainly didn't think, when she was working so hard on her dance essays, that she would end up writing a book like this one! Now it's time for you to put the book down and get on with writing your own chapter in dance history. Please keep us informed of your progress, and whatever direction your dancing takes, enjoy every step of the way. If this book has helped to make your journey easier, we'll be dancing for joy right alongside you!

Case Studies

Two working dancers

Having broken down the building of a dance career into basic steps both on and offstage, we wanted to share with you the career stories of two very different dancers. Each one is outstanding in their own field; in fact, each is outstanding in *several fields*. But in each story you should be able to see the basic principles that you have been reading about in these pages at work. And as you observe how they have led to success in the careers of Honey Kalaria and Nick Winston, don't forget to ask yourself how *you* can use them to fulfil your own dance dreams.

Honey Kalaria is the Queen of Bollywood dance in Britain ... but that is just one aspect of a career which includes acting, filmmaking, judging Channel 4 TV's *Bollywood Star* show and a wide variety of charity work. However, it is as a successful businesswoman that any aspiring dancer – regardless of their particular specialism – can learn from Honey's approach and attitude.

> I am someone who has always had a passion for dance. I love movement, I love expression and I love music. Not a day goes past without me being involved in this area. I will be choreographing a dance routine, or organising a show, perhaps writing a script for a dance-related television programme, maybe giving advice to a dancer looking for work, or researching new opportunities for my students and agency members. This is everyday work for me, and although it's not always plain sailing, it is an area I feel blessed to be in. I am a solutions-orientated person and enjoy open communication with students, business associates and staff members – always having the end goal of finding a 'win-win' situation for everyone in everything I do.

My aim in life is to make a difference to this world using the dance and entertainment knowledge and skills I have been blessed with, and this is and will be my journey in life! My first taste of the limelight was at the age of four, when I won first prize in a talent competition in Malawi, Africa, which is my birthplace. After arriving in the UK it took me a few years to settle down – a time when I missed my dancing terribly. At the age of 13, I set up a girls' youth club called the Shaan Club, which was supported by the Asian Women's Association based in Ilford. At a charity event all members of the Shaan Club took part by performing dances. It was my very first show in the UK! Immediately, I was approached and booked by a promoter to perform in Norway. I had now entered the World of Entertainment!

I thoroughly enjoyed dancing and started attending classes in disco and rock-and-roll. Other forms I have been trained in include Indian classical, belly dancing and Latin American. During my school summer holidays, whilst all my friends would go out and play, I would fly off to India to learn classical dancing. It was a rigorous training schedule, as I would train for more than six hours a day, seven days a week, all through my holiday. This taught me how to be disciplined, remain focused and have sheer determination – qualities that I continue to develop and implement in everyday life. For example, whilst studying for my Masters degree in Stirling I wanted to continue my dancing, so I would fly down to London *every* weekend, perform three or four shows and return to begin a week of intensive studying again. In addition, I have won first prize in every single dance competition that I have ever entered. Oh yes, except one – the UK Latin American Dance Championships, where I came fourth.

One of the reasons I decided to study for a MSc in Public Relations was to study effective communication between various cultures. I love the idea of a multicultural society and enjoy learning about customs, culture and diversity. I have close friends from different areas of the world including Japan, Greece, Spain, Bombay and Zimbabwe. I am proud to be a British Asian living in the

UK, as I have had the privilege of receiving the best of both the Eastern and Western culture. Again this has a direct effect on me as I promote my East-West work.

I promoted the idea of East-West dancing from the early 1990s, when I set up an East-West dance troupe called Honey, Sunny and the Diva Dancers. This comprised five Western dancers trained in ballet, modern jazz and tap, as well as Sunny and myself. I choreographed dances and trained the group to perform to Bollywood, Bhangra and Indian classical dance songs at events and functions nationally and internationally. At a later date, the skills and practical experience obtained over the years resulted in me receiving the title of the UK's principal Modern Indian Dance expert.

I have had the opportunity to use my East-West dance skills to choreograph pop videos, including one for Kula Shaker, concerts for mainstream bands such as Soul to Soul, feature films like *Bollywood Queen* and Bollywood concerts catering for audiences made up of tens of thousands. Choreographing Bollywood concerts at the age of 16 allowed me to build contacts in this field and acquire valuable knowledge that is still useful in my current work. Hard work always pays off!

I conducted intensive research to discover how I could use my skills and be of service to the community. The time was well invested as I found that there was a niche in the market. British Asians wanted to learn to dance to Bollywood music; they did not want to learn Indian traditional dancing but at the same time did not want to completely lose their cultural identity. From this was born the idea of launching a British Asian Dance Academy and providing the highest quality of training in Modern Indian Arts. It looked like God was on my side!

I have stored away in my memory, inspiring stories and wise teachings by others. I recall receiving full support from my mother, who would take me to all my shows and teach me how to behave, communicate and negotiate with organisers. I remember a wonderful old wise man telling me that on your way up, you must always remember to take others with you. It can get pretty lonely and life can become meaningless, if you forget the very same people who have encouraged you to move forwards. Another memorable saying was that you must always go up a step at a time, as any hasty moves or shortcuts can bring you crashing back down! Do things and do them well. Now, I try to pass on these great teachings to my students. All the practical knowledge that I have gained and experienced over the years is the greatest wealth that I possess, and one which I believe can be of tremendous value to others!

In 1988 I lost my sister, Preeti, and two friends in a car crash. I broke my jaw, shoulder and ankle and received major head and facial injuries. It was a very challenging time for the whole family. Preeti was a beautiful soul and an extremely good dancer. We both used to discuss at great lengths how we would use our dance skills to help others when we grew up. Some of my current dreams and ambitions were *our* dreams and ambitions, and through my work in the field of dance I am working towards fulfilling them step by step. I never take my life for granted, and have learnt to live each day as if it were my last! You achieve a lot more this way!

In memory of my sister, I set up the PSP Charity Fund. The aim was to raise money in memory of the three young people, and to donate the funds to worthwhile causes. I would organise each annual show which catered for 700–800 people, from booking the artists and venues, inviting special guests and liaising with the media, right through to arranging publicity and performing myself. It was fun but tough going as a teenaged student! However, it always seemed worthwhile as thousands of people benefited from the funds raised. I also managed to donate a mobile eye hospital to Bihar, India, allowing help to be provided to sick people in remote villages. I have regularly taken an active role in charity and fundraising events; I have also been involved in a charity parachute jump and helped to raise more than £60,000. To date, I have raised more than £1,000,000 for charity by organising and taking part in fundraising events. It's amazing how even small contributions end up making a huge difference!

Setting up Honey's Dance Academy and seeing it benefit so many people has brought great joy to me. In just four years, student numbers have grown from 22 to over 700; the dance classes are hugely popular. From launching one school, seven schools are now being run throughout London with many people on the waiting list wishing to join. Additional classes could easily be introduced if more high-quality teachers were available in the UK, but with no previous training available here for Modern Indian Arts this has proved to be a difficult task. As my main objective is to offer the highest quality of training, I refuse to compromise the standards of tuition on offer. Dance enthusiasts who are keen to teach are currently undergoing a three-year teacher training programme, with an offer of guaranteed full-time employment upon completion. In this way we can maintain the highest quality and standards. The students' best interests are always high on the agenda!

Students are always encouraged to take part in shows, films and other projects. I find that this is one of the best ways of helping them boost their confidence, develop interpersonal and team-building skills, raise self-esteem and promote their health and fitness levels. As an added benefit, students' performing skills tend to improve more rapidly and it also allows them to get involved in arts and cultural activities. Our academy has received many letters of thanks from parents, students, events organisers and audience members for our efforts, the quality of the students' performances and for providing such opportunities.

Based on the excellent benefits and cultural value of Modern Indian Arts, my mission is now to educate and inform people from all backgrounds – Asians or non-Asians – about the two most popular Modern Indian Dance forms, Bollywood and Bhangra. With the recent interest in Indian cinema, Bollywood is becoming immensely popular with non-Asians. This has been witnessed by the rise in numbers of non-Asians attending classes. Furthermore, I have been inundated with requests by arts organisations, theatre groups and dance forums to conduct Bollywood and Bhangra dance workshops and lectures.

It is encouraging to see that if Modern Indian Dance forms were made available to a larger audience, many more people would be able to enjoy and benefit from the art form. Requests to conduct workshops for the mainstream market are increasing day by day. Some already booked include a one-day workshop to be held in Ireland and one to be held in Olympia for a dance exhibition, which normally attracts 40,000 people. Even Bollywood productions being filmed in the UK are asking for Western dancers to perform to Bollywood songs. As I write this, we will be providing more than 300 artists for a Bollywood film to be shot in London from which 40 are Western dancers booked for a whole month.

For the past two years I have been creating a Modern Indian Dance syllabus to allow professional accreditation to be offered to students and teachers. My aim is to set up a recognised professional body called IAMIA (International Association of Modern Indian Arts) and provide worldwide recognised accreditation to qualified members. It has been an interesting task, as no such syllabus has ever been compiled in the past. It will be a historical event, when launched!

I continuously strive to offer my service to the best of my ability and to work towards reaching my full potential, whilst encouraging others to do the same. My aim in life is to make a difference to the world, starting from my family and moving out to my workplace, dance schools, local communities, regions, countries and then expanding worldwide. To do well, everything takes time and effort, but that does not deter me. Anything worthwhile in life is worth working for. I want to enjoy my journey through life and share the joy of living with others.

Honey's drive to dance, work and live to the best of her ability are echoed in the story of award-winning dancer **Nick Winston**. Here is the story of his journey from top performer to respected and much-in-demand choreographer and director:

My first school was Parkside Academy in my home town of Northampton. It was a small private school that also taught dance, and by the age of four I was joining in. Aged eight I successfully auditioned for the Young London Ballet Company that rehearsed on weekends in London. We performed a new piece called 'Pedro The Parrot' at the Saddlers Wells Theatre, based on the children's book by Jill Tookey. Talent scouts came to rehearsals and from that I was chosen to appear at the London Coliseum with Rudolf Nureyev and the Boston Ballet company in *Don Quixote*. Although I didn't really enjoy ballet, I understood that it was the foundation of good technique and at 11, my parents took me to audition for the Royal Ballet Company. Much to my surprise I was accepted and left home to board at White Lodge and begin my training for the company. I hated every minute of it and quit after three weeks, returning home and to Parkside. I've never regretted the decision and never looked back.

Over the next five years I appeared at the Royal Theatre in Northampton in musicals, plays and pantomimes, and fell in love with working in the theatre. I won a scholarship to train at RAD (the Royal Academy of Dance) and my father and I travelled every Saturday morning to Battersea for my tuition. I continued to do the dance festivals, now choreographing my own routines. At 16 I won the Jessie Mathews Choreography Award, a national event that unfortunately now no longer exists.

I began my colleague training at Laine Theatre Arts in 1990 and whilst studying there appeared in two Royal Variety performances, two pantomimes and several fashion shows. Much to the dismay of the principal, I left after my second year to move to Hamburg and appear in Andrew Lloyd Webber's *Cats*. I stayed in the show for two years, performing the role of Plato/Macavity and Alonzo/

Rumpus. I left to appear in the German production of *Starlight Express* in Bochum but during rehearsals was offered the European premiere of Disney's *Beauty and the Beast* in Vienna and skated out of there.

During rehearsals for *Beauty and the Beast* I was offered the position of Dance Captain by the Broadway choreographer, Matt West. I was thrilled and really enjoyed my 18 months with the show. When the show moved to the West End, Matt made me his Assistant Choreographer. It was during auditions for the show that I met my wife Laura-Michelle Kelly. Also whilst working on the show I began to choreograph again, working on various charity shows and at several London colleagues. Although doors were beginning to open up in this direction, there were still things I wanted to achieve as a performer and I focused my attention on that.

After another 18 months with *Beauty*, I joined the London cast of *Chicago* as Fred Casely, with Maria Friedman and later Chita Rivera. Choreographic work kept presenting itself and I worked on Paul Mitchell hair shows in London and Paris.

My next West End production was *Fosse* at the Prince Of Wales Theatre, performing among other things the number 'Steam Heat' and singing 'Mr Bojangles'. During my time on this show I choreographed the 25th Anniversary performance of *Side By Side By Sondheim*, which reunited the original cast (Julie Mackenzie, David Kernan, Millicent Martin and Ned Sherrin) as well as featuring many stars including Dame Cleo Lane. The director, David Kernan, then asked me to choreograph a new show entitled *Dorothy Fields Forever* about the female lyricist who wrote *Sweet Charity* and *Seesaw*. The show played at the Jerymn Street theatre and was a success. It returned to that venue later on in the same year, prior to a four-month run at the King's Head Theatre.

After *Fosse* I was invited to return to *Chicago* for six months, now starring Denise Van Outen. From there I joined the original cast of *Kiss Me Kate* at the London Victoria, playing Grumio and understudying Bill Calhohn for more than 70 performances. During that time I choreographed the musicals *Dames At Sea*, *Pirates Of Penzance* and *A Slice Of Saturday Night* for Mountview Theatre colleague. The director of the latter was Hannah Chissick, who during our rehearsals was appointed Artistic Director of Harrogate Theatre.

Broadway director Moni Yakem, who had seen *Dorothy Fields Forever*, invited me to choreograph his new show *Let Us Fly*, also at the King's Head Theatre. Starring Dave Willits, this show was a moderate success and played for six weeks. Shortly afterwards I choreographed a 'gardening cabaret' at the Jerymn Street theatre called *Natural Filth* ... and yes, it was as bizarre as it sounds.

After *Kiss Me Kate* (which was recorded and released on DVD) I appeared as Riff in *West Side Story* at the Leicester Haymarket, and as Bobby Van Hussen in the 50th Anniversary production of *The Boyfriend* at the Theatre Royal in Windsor and its subsequent tour. After ten years treading the boards, this was my swan song as a performer. I went back to Mountview to choreograph *A, My Name Is Alice*, but unfortunately the director became very ill during rehearsals and I ended up directing the show. It was something I had always wanted to do, but – like my reluctance to choreograph before my performing demons were exorcised – I thought I wouldn't be directing for another ten years.

I then joined Hannah Chissick in Harrogate to choreograph *Aladdin*, *Side By Side By Sondheim*, and to co-direct with her the Fats Waller musical *Ain't Misbehavin'* which starred Ray Shell. Now I have just completed directing and choreographing *Starting Here, Starting Now* at Mountview, before working on another show there, *Jerry's Girls*. After that it's back to Harrogate for the Sondheim revue, *Putting It Together* and the Pantomime *Mother Goose*. Then Hannah and I will head to Stoke to put on their panto, *Cinderella* with Lisa Riley.

These opportunities would not have arrived if it weren't for my work in colleagues and at charity shows. I don't think it matters where you begin – if your work is good, doors will open for you. It really is other people's faith in me that has led to me directing, even though it has always been and remains my true ambition (and of course a healthy dose of encouragement from my wife hasn't hurt either).

As you start out on (or perhaps move on to the next step of) your own dance journey, you may well experience even more varied career moves than Honey or Nick. Whatever opportunities or challenges life throws at you, do bear in mind the common threads of commitment, hard work and a constant drive to get better and try new things that mark the career stories of both these successful dancers.

With a Little Help From My Friends

A resource for the working dancer

For a medium that doesn't transfer very well to the printed page, there is an incredible variety of dance resources available in print and increasingly on the Internet. There is certainly no reason why, between jobs, you shouldn't be exercising your mind as much as your body: in fact such research and learning can only help that individual career vision we have spoken about in the body of this book. The following is a selection of resources that we particularly like and find useful. Bear in mind that what works for one person may not always work for another; equally, if you have a favourite resource that we haven't included here, by all means let us know and we will include a link in our next edition.

Dance books

High Kicks: the essential guide to working as a dancer by Donna Ross
Particularly strong in pulling together the experiences of many working dancers, as told in their own words, and built on the solid foundation of Donna's own experience and expertise.

An Applicant's Guide to Auditioning and Interviewing at Dance and Drama Schools (Council for Dance Education and Training, 2002)
Published by the Council for Dance Education and Training, this guide gives practical and realistic advice about how to choose the right course – and just as important, how to apply for it once you have found it. Written by professionals, it also includes useful insights from students already attending dance schools.

Dance Masters: interviews with legends of dance by Janet Lynn Roseman (*Routledge, 2001*)
If you're aiming for the top, it's best to get advice from the top. This book features interviews, bios and photos from some very big names.

The Oxford Dictionary of Dance edited by Debra Craine & Judith Mackrell (*Oxford University Press, 2000*)
Even if you specialise in street dance, you need to know your craft – and that means knowing the terms which are used to describe it. There are very few terms, from the ballet world to the Hollywood musical, that you won't find described clearly and concisely here.

Dance Composition (fifth edition) by Jacqueline Smith-Autard (*A & C Black, 2004*)
An essential book for anyone with ambitions as a choreographer, this has been a bestseller for more than 20 years.

Laban for Actors and Dancers by Jean Newlove (*Nick Hern Books, 1993*)
It has been said that Laban is to movement what Stanislavski is to acting. He devised the first wholly successful system for recording human movement, a system which is increasingly influential in training not just dancers, but anyone who wants to work on the physicality of their performance. Jean Newlove was Rudolf Laban's first assistant in England and this handbook is written from a lifetime of experience. It guides students through the use of space, time and what Laban identified as the 'Eight Basic Actions'. Each chapter comes complete with easy-to-follow exercises.

As a working dancer we would also encourage you to look further than just the dance section of the library for your inspiration. In particular, we recommend that you keep an eye on bestselling business and personal development books: Stephen Coveney's *Seven Habits of Highly Effective People* and Dale Carnegie's *The Power of Positive Thinking*, for example. Besides helping you in other aspects of your life, you could do yourself a lot of good by thinking specifically about how the principles contained in these books could be applied to your dancing career. We particularly recommend *Your Best Year Yet* by Jinny Ditzler (published by Thorsons), which is not so much a book as a three-hour life-planning workshop to help you balance your dancing goals with the rest of your activities and responsibilities. It will quite possibly be the most important three hours you spend all year.

Dance publications and websites

CyberDance:Ballet on the Net
www.cyberdance.org
Almost 4000 classical ballet and modern dance links.

Dance Europe Magazine
www.danceeurope.net
A good way to get an overview of dance activities and opport-unities away from home.

Dance Magazine
www.dancemagazine.com
Established since 1927, *Dance Magazine* is one of the world's most authoritative dance publications. The website allows you to browse old issues and lists many special publications and resources which, while centred on the US market, are of use to any serious dancer worldwide.

Dance Teacher
www.danceteacher.com
A comprehensive American website and magazine resource for dance teachers, covering the career and artistic side in great detail. You can also find sections on cheerleading to give you another string to your dance bow!

Dance Web
www.danceweb.co.uk
Packed with information for UK dance enthusiasts, both profes-sional and amateur.

Database of the Library of Paris' Cité de la Musique
www.cite-musique.fr
More than 28,000 documents on dance and music, including scores, books, magazines, documentaries and videos.

International Dance Council (UNESCO)
www.unesco.org
Dance links and contacts.

Institute for Historical Dance Practice
www.historicaldance.com
Research on dance from the 15th to the 19th century.

London Dance
www.londondance.com
A comprehensive listing of dance events and news in London –
but worth checking out even if you live somewhere else in the
country!

Off Jazz Dance World
www.offjazz.com
Jazz dance and tap dancing site. History, terminology, intern-
ships, documentation, and demonstration videos.

Talent Box
www.talentbox.com
Very strong on niche-market type dance sites.

Worldwide Dance Pages Directory
www.newdance.com
Contemporary companies and choreographers.

www.ballet.co.uk
A huge resource for ballet folk – updated almost daily.

www.ballroomdancers.com
A resource for the strictly ballroom set – with additional items
of interest to swing dance aficionados.

www.danceonline.com
International site – new dance.

www.dancer.com
Although this website is run by the Gaynor Minden company to
promote its range of dance shoes, it features good advice on the
dancer's health and fitness – including the opportunity to ask
questions of medical experts via e-mail.

www.dancetimepublications.com
This site focuses on social dancing, and sells lots of rare and instructive footage of great and famous dancers in action.

www.dansenet.com
News, events, list of companies, teaching, information.

www.folkdancing.com
A comprehensive source of information on dances from most regions of the world. Whatever 'river' your latest dance project flows from, you should find a good starting point for your research here.

www.irishdancer.co.uk
A site that does exactly what it says on the tin!

www.ladanse.com
European dance Internet site with a list of companies, events, venues, an e-zine and a newsletter.

www.vocalist.org.uk
Without doubt the brightest and most comprehensive site for singers in the UK. Tons of useful information for everyone from the 'hobbyist' to the seasoned professional, and certainly a great resource for any dancer looking to brush up on the vocal side of their talents.

Dance organisations

Equity
www.equity.org.uk
Although Equity is often considered to be the actor's union, membership includes performers of every sort, working as individuals or as groups in pubs, clubs and other light entertainment venues, pop, theatre, television, films and in places of worship. Dancers are covered in all of the following Equity Agreements:

- National and house agreements for opera
- West End, provincial, subsidised repertory and small-scale theatre agreements
- BBC, ITV and PACT television agreements

- CORCA agreement for variety artists
- PACT cinema agreement
- TV commercials guidelines

Equity also aims to represent members working abroad (on cruise ships, for instance) and, even if a member is engaged on a non-Equity contract, is happy to give advice. The union has a specialist Choreographers' Committee, and Equity's Regional Organisers are also well-versed in issues affecting dancers, so help and information are never far away.

Council for Dance Education and Training (CDET)

Toynbee Hall, 28 Commercial Street, London E1 6LS
Tel: 020 7247 4030 Fax: 020 7247 3404
Answers for dancers: 0901 8800014
Email: "mailto:info@cdet.org.uk"
The Council for Dance Education and Training (CDET) promotes excellence in dance education and training. It accredits courses at vocational dance schools, advocates on behalf of the private dance training and teaching communities, and provides a comprehensive information service about dance education and training. CDET offers advice and support to students, parents, teachers and artists; it also informs the work of government and other agencies working in dance.

The International Dance Teachers Association (IDTA)

International House, 76 Bennett Road, Brighton, East Sussex BN2 5JL
Tel: +44 (0)1273 685652 Fax: +44 (0)1273 674388
Email: "mailto:info@idta.co.uk"
The IDTA provides a wide range of examination services that have been established over time and meet the needs of the public, the professional performer and the teaching community. The IDTA is a government-accredited QCA body and continues to work with the various government agencies and representative bodies in order to keep abreast of current trends and indeed, influence the progress of dance.

The Samaritans
Always on call 24 hours a day, completely confidential, and contacted by many more dancers – both unknown and world-famous – than you might imagine. National numbers: in the UK dial 08457 90 90 90, for the cost of a local call. In the Republic of Ireland dial 1850 60 90 90, for the cost of a local call. There also local branches and a website: **www.samaritans.co.uk.**

Consumer Credit Counselling Service
A free and confidential service that will help you regain control of your finances. Tel: 0800 138 1111; website: **www.cccs.co.uk.**

Josh Image Consultancy
91–95 Church St, Croyden, Surrey CR0 1RN
Tel: 020 8649 8919
Many image consultancies offer a 'full range of services', from hair and make-up advice to clothes and styling. The Josh organisation, based in Croydon in the UK, goes one step further, offering confidential counselling by trained professionals with a particular interest in performance and music. Mention this book and you will get a discount on the initial consultation fee.

If you can't find what you're looking for in any of the above, try these 'gateway' sites which will lead you to many separate categories of dance-related information. If you *still* can't find the site you're looking for, maybe it's time you started it yourself!

Artslynx
www.artslynx.org

World Wide Arts Resources
http://wwar.com
Search engine and servers classified by dance style.

Nigel Grant's website
Nigel Grant has many years of experience in helping dancers make the transition from full-time performing to other areas. Nigel's website provides much useful information at: **www.dtol.ndirect.co.uk.**

Nigel also runs courses, a good example being 'Making the Transition from Dancer to Manager'. This extended three-day course is for dancers and ex-dancers who want to broaden their outlook to encompass new ways of thinking and behaving. Check this out if you want to develop your career and prepare for a career in management, particularly (but not exclusively) in dance companies or schools.

John Byrne's website
www.showbusinesslifecoach.com
John's site (through which you can also contact Jenny) includes lots of useful information and resources for performers, such as an online tool to help clarify your career vision and the chance to book a free coaching session with John or one of his team.

Contributors' websites
Below are the websites of some of the dance experts who have contributed to this book. In addition to providing further information, the sites will give you some inspiration for creating a site of your own.

Jacquie Bird: www.dtol.ndirect.co.uk/p607.htm
Brenda Bufalino: www.brendabufalino.com
Deborah Greenfield: www.rosanegraflamenco.org
David Watson: www.cremecube.com

Index